LIFE · EARTH · PHYSICAL

DIRT-CHEAP SCIENCE

ACTIVITY-BASED UNITS
GAMES, EXPERIMENTS
& REPRODUCIBLES
BY ESTHER WEINER

SCHOLASTIC
PROFESSIONAL BOOKS

New York · Toronto · London · Auckland · Sydney

Dedication

This book is dedicated to the following people who helped me discover and refine my interest in science education for young children: My parents; the Science Museum of Long Island; the children, supportive staff, and administration of the E. M. Baker School, Great Neck, New York; and finally, my husband Howard and our two children, Michael and Jonathan, who tolerated and participated in many beginning "experiments" in our kitchen.

Designed by Nancy Metcalf
Production by Intergraphics
Cover design by Vincent Cici
Cover illustration by Mona Mark
Illustrations by Michelle Fridkin, Nancy Metcalf

ISBN 0-590-49138-5

Contents

Part One: Life Science

Be a Tree Detective

Leaf Tic Tac Toe (Game)

Inside Leaf Patterns

Leafy Treasure Hunt

Ring Around the Plant World (Game)

Overhead and Underfoot Walk
Woods Systems Sleuth

Squirmy Science

String Toss: A Mini-Ecology Study

Eat Your Way Through Botany (Mini-Unit)

Contents (cont.)

Part Two: Earth Science
Air: A Weighty Topic

Air: It Matters to Us All!

The System We Live On—Planet Earth
Part 1: Can Soil (a Solid) Hold Air (a Gas)?

The System We Live On—Planet Earth
Part 2: Can Water (a Liquid) Hold Air (a Gas)?

The System We Live On—Planet Earth
Part 3: What Can Make Molecules Jump?

The Love Life of Water Molecules

Contents (cont.)

Contents (cont.)

Introduction

This book is based upon lessons I conduct at the E. M. Baker School. I always begin the school year with botany—no matter what grade I am working with, in my role as Science Consultant for the school. Why begin with botany?

Sylvia Earle, the first woman to be chief scientist at the National Oceanic and Atmospheric Administration, was featured and quoted as saying in the June 23, 1991, *New York Times Magazine* article entitled "Champion of the Deep": "If you study plants you look at everything—geology, chemistry of the environment. Plants are the energy base for the whole system. A tree is not a tree by itself. It hosts jillions of creatures—birds, insects, fungi. Botany leads to the universe."

That is the basic purpose of this book: to lead students to discover the Universe.

The ability to recognize patterns, transfer information, make connections and, finally, understand systems is what elementary science—life, earth, and physical—should be about. The lessons in this book attempt to lead children to discover that everything affects everything, because the world really is one great system.

I have tried to make this a cohesive, sequential book—not just a compilation of science activities. The lessons are arranged in the order I would follow in the classroom, though they do not necessarily have to be used in that way. Many of the activities can be reused several times during the year.

Nearly all of the activities are planned for cooperative groups of children. I find that the activities generally work best with groups of four, and that is the size I recommend unless another number is specified. You may, of course, find that groups of a different size work best with your students.

Several of the data sheets follow a format based loosely upon the "scientific method." If you are working with very young children, it may be more appropriate for you to use the data sheets as a basis for experience charts. All activities can be used for all grades. Expository writing skills can be practiced when older grades write hypotheses, observations, and conclusions.

To make some of the data sheets easier to follow for younger grades, a symbol such as a triangle has been placed next to each section in the data sheet. It is easier for younger readers to find the section if you say, "Put your finger on the triangle" rather than, "Look for the hypothesis."

Classroom management, background information, and strategic tips have been included in each lesson, so you don't have to flip back and forth trying to find what you need. In a few lessons the background information has been placed in a separate section for clarity. Elsewhere it has been woven into the Procedures sections so it is at your fingertips.

Finally, don't be dismayed by the unexpected. Experiments may not always work as planned, especially when the weather or some other condition beyond your control is unsuitable. In any case, you can take advantage of mistakes— for example, by asking the children to help you in the detective work of finding out what went wrong.

What I love about my job is discovering new science connections along with my students. I hope you enjoy the same experience with yours!

l i f e

Be A Tree Detective

Recommended for Grades K–2 as an opening lesson and Grades 3–4 as a review

Lesson Overview

A simple classification activity with tree leaves and bark is followed (in the same session or a later one) by an outdoor detective walk. The two activities will allow children to discover these . . .

Science Principles

1. Living things have properties that help them survive.
2. Bark protects trees much as skin and feathers protect animals.
3. Bark and leaf patterns can be unique and thus help identify the tree.

Materials Needed

1. Brown chalk.
2. Double-stick tape.
3. Extra copies of the data sheet (as many as there are student groups).
4. A selection of peeled crayons.

Optional

5. A tree cookie (slice of tree trunk with bark attached). If possible, one for each group. You may be able to get this from a firewood vendor or tree surgeon.
7. Some down feathers.
8. Samples of snake skin.

For each group

9. One paper plate.

For each child

10. Data sheet.

Getting Started

1. Before class, cut out the leaf samples from the group copies of the data sheet, and keep them in sets.

   Use the sheet as is if you have a sweet gum, beech, and maple (Norway or sugar) on or near your school property. If not, sketch leaves from other species near your school, and paste your sketches over the existing drawings.

   On the board, use brown chalk to draw three tree trunks with several branches. Make sure the branches are within the children's reach. Add a different bark pattern (e.g. mottled, striped, dotted) to each trunk.

   Place double-stick tape on the branches where children will put their leaves. There should be at least as many pieces of tape as there are children.

2. Begin the lesson by allowing the children to feel the bark on the tree cookies and the feathers and snakeskin, if you have them. In any case, ask the brainstorming question: *What do feathers, skin, and tree bark have in common?*

   Try to elicit if they are found on the outside or inside of living things. After establishing that they are found on the outside, ask: *Why do you think animals have skin, scales, hair, or feathers?*

Lead the children to understand that bark protects the inside of the tree from weather and animal (insect) intrusion, the way skin, etc., protects animals from weather and germs.

3. Draw the children's attention to the bare trees on the board. Ask what important parts of the trees are missing from the branches.

When the children have identified the leaves as missing, inform them that the leaves are important because they manufacture the trees' food. (Sugar, through the process of photosynthesis.)

4. Ask the children if the trees are all the same kind. Have them explain why or why not. Be sure to elicit a description of the different bark patterns. Then ask if the children think the trees would all have leaves of the same kind.

Pre-Walk Activity

 Procedure

1. Spread the paper leaf samples on the paper plates.
2. Ask for volunteers to select and place leaves on the trees.
3. The first volunteer may select any leaf and place it on any tree.
4. The second and third children must choose different leaves and place them on different trees.
5. Other children may choose any leaf but must place it on its matching tree.
6. Continue until every child has had an opportunity to place a leaf.

 Strategic Tips

1. To keep all children involved, ask them to give a thumbs-up or thumbs-down on each leaf placement. This will also allow you to assess classification skills.

Outdoor Detective Walk

 Procedure

1. Tell the children they are going outside to look for trees that best match the leaves drawn on their data sheets.
2. Grab a bag of peeled crayons and have the children take their data sheets. Then head for the trees.
3. When your children discover a matching tree, have them feel the texture of the bark. Then have them create a bark rubbing in the appropriate space on the data sheet. Show them how to place the sheet against the trunk and rub the side of the crayon on the paper.
4. Challenge the children to find all the trees in the area which have matching bark. They should look at the leaves only to double-check the identifications.
5. Repeat steps 3 and 4 with the other two tree species.

 Strategic Tips

1. Change crayon colors for each rubbing.
2. Have older students write descriptions of bark patterns and challenge each other to find the tree being described.

l   i   f   e

Tree Detective

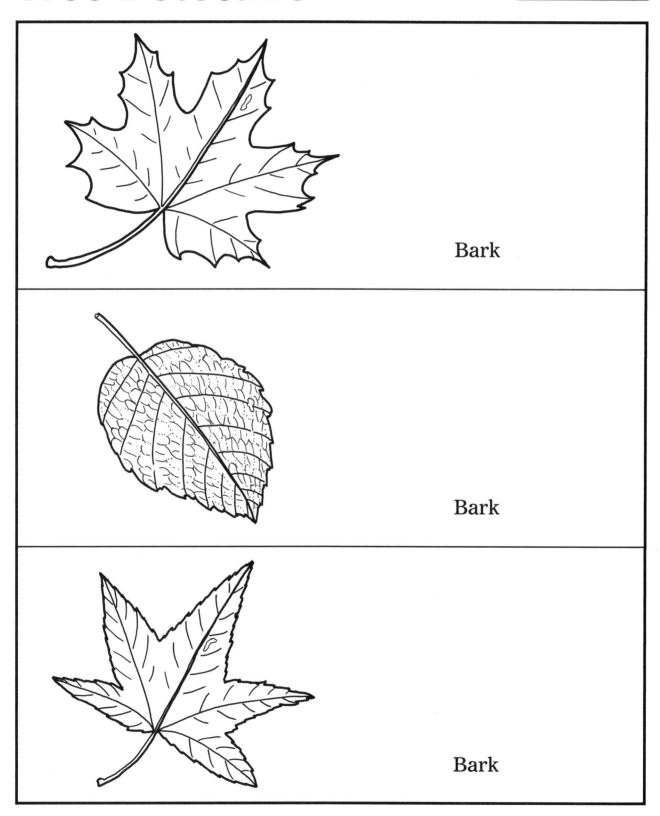

Bark

Bark

Bark

Leaf Tic Tac Toe

Recommended for Grades K–4

Lesson Overview

Classifying leaf shapes and vein patterns, and playing a team game of tic tac toe, will give your students a cooperative learning experience while reinforcing these . . .

Science Principles

1. Leaves have physical properties which enable us to identify them.

2. These physical properties enable the leaves to perform certain functions; e.g. the shape of a leaf may enable it to funnel rain water into the soil beneath the plant.

3. Leaves from the same tree will vary in size depending on age or position on the tree. For example, because a seedling needs large quantities of sugar in order to grow, its leaves may be very large.

Materials Needed

For each group

1. One 9-square tic tac toe board. (Make it out of tagboard, with squares large enough to accommodate your leaves.)

2. A collection of five leaves from each of four varieties (20 leaves in all). If real leaves are unavailable, make copies of dicot leaves from Ring Around the Plant World (pages 26–30). Make an extra set for yourself

3. One plastic bag.

Getting Started

1. Before class, prepare the boards and leaf collections and place each collection in a plastic bag.

2. Tell the children that they are going to play a new game called tic tac toe. Of course, they'll groan and inform you that they are all experts at it.

3. Explain that old-fashioned tic tac toe requires strategic skills of blocking your opponent to win, but now they are going to play a cooperative team game in which they try *not* to block their teammates.

4. The object of the game is for each team to try to get three leaves of one kind in a row (or column or diagonal), instead of Xs or Os.

5. Each child in the group will be in charge of one leaf variety.

6. Tell the children that you will start with a practice game.

Procedure

1. Distribute the boards and leaf collections to the teams. Give each child a specific leaf from his/her team's bag. Have the children empty the remainder of their bags gently on top of the board. Each child then selects his/her own pile of matching leaves.

2. Select a leaf at random from your collection and hold it up.

Tell the children to decide who has the matching leaf on their team.

3. The child with the leaf will place it on the board. First, however, encourage the members of the team to discuss the best placement. Have them consider the probability of three leaves of the same kind being selected in succession.

4. Inform the children that you will not replace your selected leaves in the bag, so the odds will keep changing during the game.

5. Make it clear that once you hold up a new leaf, the children may not change the position of any leaf already on the board.

6. Continue selecting leaves until a team wins.

7. After a win, you can extend the game by challenging the teams to see if they can get two rows of matching leaves. The losing teams now have a chance to overtake the winner.

8. You can vary the game by describing each leaf's properties before you display it, so that the children practice auditory as well as visual discrimination skills.

Strategic Tips

1. Your class level should determine the four varieties of leaves you pick. For upper grades, you can use properties such as teeth or vein patterns, rather than shape, for your classification categories.

2. Plan to repeat the activity. Increased practice will sharpen the children's classification and strategic thinking skills.

3. To preserve the leaves between games, sprinkle each team's collection with a few drops of water and store it in its plastic bag.

Inside Leaf Patterns
Hunting on Your Own for Patterns
(followup)

Inside Leaf Patterns is *recommended for Grades K–2 as a culminating classification lesson, and for Grades 3–4 as an introductory lesson.*

Hunting on Your Own For Patterns is *recommended for Grades 1–3.*

 Lesson Overview

The children identify and classify leaves by observing vein patterns. The discussion of these patterns should branch out into a discussion of other types of patterns found in nature, as children discover these . . .

 Science Principles

1. The parts of plants have properties that enable them to survive. A leaf has veins which carry water in and sugar (produced in the leaf) out.

2. A *pinnate* vein pattern looks like a feather pattern inside the leaf, while a *palmate* vein pattern resembles fingers radiating from a palm. The veins in a palmate leaf radiate from its stem (petiole).

3. In a *parallel* vein pattern, the veins run side by side from stem to tip. Grasses and lily of the valley display this pattern, for example. (It is not necessary to volunteer this particular information during the lesson.)

 Materials Needed

1. A small collection of real leaves. This should consist of a few palmate leaves and one pinnate leaf (e.g. several maple leaves and one oak leaf).

For each group
2. A collection of paper leaves cut from copies of samples in Ring Around the Plant World (pages 26–30).

3. A paper plate.

For each child
4. Data sheet and (if you plan to use it) followup sheet.

 Getting Started

1. Before class, place each group's leaf collection on a paper plate.

2. Draw some geometric patterns on the board and ask for volunteers to extend them. Include a pinnate design alternating with a palmate design, but without the leaf's outline.

2. Ask the children if they think the veins of leaves might come in patterns, too. Distribute the leaf collections and ask the children to look through the leaves to see if they notice any repeating designs in the veins.

 Procedure

1. Introduce the data sheet, and take the children step by step.

2. Have the children fill in the conclusion. Tell them that the patterns they detected have special names that will help them remember what the pattern itself looks like. (See Science Principles #2.)
3. To check for understanding, challenge the class to identify an oak leaf (for example) by finding the only pinnate leaf in your collection of real leaves.
4. Use Hunting on Your Own for Patterns as a followup.

Hunting on Your Own for Patterns

 Procedure

1. Distribute copies of the followup data sheet. Make sure the children understand what is required for the prediction, method, observation, and conclusion.
2. Have the children survey an area near either the school or their home to see what leaf patterns are present.

 Strategic Tips

1. If you have deciduous trees in your area, this lesson is best conducted in the fall. The fall color changes illustrate the cycle of the seasons and show how living things can react to those changes. Also, leaf veins will become beautifully apparent in leaves that are decomposing.
2. Do not introduce the parallel pattern until you are certain that the children can distinguish between pinnate and palmate—or until a child asks you if there are other patterns. It's much more exciting for them to discover a new vein pattern themselves!

3. Here the children begin to learn plant classifications that will play an important part in subsequent lessons. You may wish to introduce parts of the following Background Information as it seems appropriate.
4. Review the symbols $<$, $>$, and $=$.

 Background Information

1. Plants with pinnate or palmate vein patterns are *dicots*, having two seed leaves. Plants with parallel vein patterns are *monocots*, having a single seed leaf.
2. Both dicots and monocots are flowering plants (*angiosperms*). They differ from plants such as conifers that have seeds but no flowers (*gymnosperms*).
3. Other plants do not have flowers or seeds. These plants include ferns and mosses.

Inside Leaf Patterns

l i f e

Patterns can give you clues which help identify objects.

Patterns repeat and repeat and _____.

▲ **PROBLEM:** Do leaves have more than one vein pattern?

▼ **HYPOTHESIS:** _____

● **METHOD:**

1. Examine your leaf collection. Can you sort it into 2 or more piles looking *only* at the veins?

2. Sketch vein patterns you detected.

☜ **OBSERVATION:**

1. I was able to sort into

   ____ pile(s).

★ **CONCLUSION:** Leaves come in ____ pattern(s).

✽ **CHALLENGE:** Do you think there are even *more* patterns?

Hunting On Your Own for Patterns!

l i f e

▲ **MY PREDICTION:** I think I will find a (circle it) > , < or = number of *pinnate* to *palmate* leaved plants.

● **METHOD:** Explore outside (or inside) your home to tally the number of pinnate or palmate plants.

☞ **OBSERVATION:** (Put your tallies in the box.)

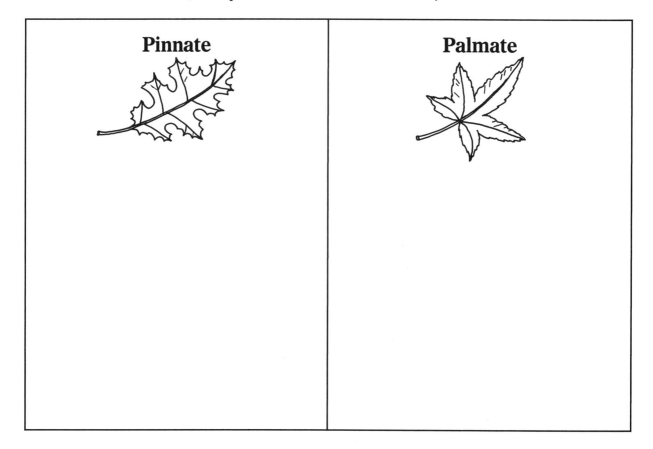

Pinnate	Palmate

★ **CONCLUSION:** Circle the correct symbol   Pinnate $\begin{matrix} > \\ < \\ = \end{matrix}$ Palmate

✳ **EXTRA:** Did you discover any other vein patterns? Sketch them.

Leafy Treasure Hunt

Recommended for Grades K–2 with the simple data sheet (page 21) or for Grades 3–4 with the advanced data sheet (page 22)

Note: Ideally, this activity should be done on school property. If there are insufficient trees around your school, plan the activity for the fall, when children can pick leaves from the ground instead of from trees.

Lesson Overview

This treasure hunt for leaves with properties matching those named on the appropriate data sheet may be spread over two or more sessions. It will lead children to discover and refine these . . .

Science Principles

1. Living things can have many adaptations (properties) that help them survive.
2. The adaptations of leaves are crucial to the plant's survival. (See Background Information for specifics.)

Materials Needed

For each group
1. A small plastic sandwich bag.
2. A larger plastic bag to contain . . .
3. A set of leaf samples (possessing the properties described on the data sheets).

For each child
4. The appropriate data sheet.

Getting Started

1. Ask the children what they think of when they hear the word "leaves." They most likely will respond with "green" or some other color word, depending on the season.
2. Inform them that leaves have many properties other than color, just as people have many distinguishing characteristics (size, shape, color, etc.).

    (It is fun for the children to discover that leaves and people have some properties with the same names—teeth, lobes, and veins!)

Procedure

1. Although the children can hunt independently, I find it is better to group them into small teams.
2. Distribute the data sheets and the bags of sample leaves.
3. Review the properties of the leaves the children are going to search for (see Background Information below). Discuss the fact (especially true of the advanced version) that some leaves may fit more than one category.
4. After the hunt, gather back in the classroom for a display and comparison of "treasures."

Background Information

Have the children look at the properties on their data sheets as you hold up and discuss the specimens you have collected.

The properties marked * below are for the advanced treasure hunt only; the one marked ** is for the simple hunt only.

a. Teeth—small projections similar to the teeth on a saw. Not all leaves have them.

b. Lobes—Larger projections which can easily be counted. Not all leaves have them.

c. Vein patterns—pinnate, palmate, or parallel. (See Inside Leaf Patterns, page 15, for more information.)

*d. Leaves can be *compound*, just as words can be compound. A compound word (such as *tree-top*) is composed of two or more shorter words. A compound leaf is composed of several leaflets all sharing the same stem.

To tell if you are looking at leaves or leaflets, check the color of the stem to which they are attached. If it is green and thin, it is most likely the stem of a compound leaf. If it is thicker and woody, it is most likely a branch with simple leaves.

*e. Both simple and compound leaves can be found growing on a branch in *opposite, alternate,* or *whorled* arrangements.

f. Some plants (gymnosperms) have *needle-like* leaves.

*g. Needle-like leaves can grow singly or in bundles. Their texture can also be used for identification. Some needles are smooth, while others look and feel like overlapping scales.

*h. Evergreen leaves remain green all year round. They can be either needles or thick, leather-like broad leaves. The thin needle shape and the thick texture each help prevent water loss over the winter.

*i. Deciduous leaves change color as they lose their chlorophyll and reveal other pigments.

**j. A spotted leaf is probably in the process of decomposing. The spots, if obviously not pigments, are mold. (This information can lead to a good discussion of the way deciduous leaves enrich the soil by decomposing each year.)

 Strategic Tips

1. Break this lesson into two or more sessions to avoid information overload.

2. Even though you are on school property, remind children not to rip off whole twigs or branches but to carefully remove one leaf per group.

3. The "treasures" may be mounted around the data sheets. Place each specimen in a clear plastic bag which is then numbered and mounted on tagboard.

4. Follow this lesson up with the Ring Around the Plant World Venn diagram game (pages 23–36).

Leafy Treasure Hunt

Find leaves that fit each of the descriptions.

teeth

1. They can have teeth.

lobes

2. They can have lobes.

3. They have vein patterns.

Palmate

Pinnate

4. They can be needles.

5. They can decompose to become part of the soil. They can have spots of mold growing on them to help this happen.

Grand Total =

l i f e

Leafy Treasure Hunt

Give yourself □ points for each found.

teeth

1. They can have teeth. □

lobes

2. They can have lobes. □

3. They can have vein patterns.

Palmate □   Pinnate □   Parallel □

4. They grow in different arrangements.

Opposite □   Alternate □   Whorled □

5. They can be simple leaves or compound leaves.

□   □

6. They can be different kinds of needles.

Scaly □   Smooth □

7. Needles can grow in different arrangements.

Singles □   Bundles □ (may come in multiples of 2, 3 or 5.)

8. They may be evergreen or deciduous.

□   □

Grand total = □

Ring Around the Plant World

Recommended for Grades 1 and 2 in its simple form and for advanced Grades 3 or 4 in its more complex form.

 Lesson Overview

This lesson should be preceded by "Leafy Treasure Hunt" (pages 19–22), in which the children become acquainted with many properties of leaves.

The team game in this lesson is based upon the organization of leaf properties in Venn diagrams. Children take turns trying to place different types of leaves in the correct classification areas on the chalkboard. This activity will give the children experience in the scientific skills of classifying, generalizing, and creating and using models in the form of charts. It will also help the children to discover these important . . .

 Science Principles

1. Organisms are classified in groups which are subsets of larger sets. When we recognize physical properties which classify an organism in a basic group, we can know that the organism also has the properties of the larger sets to which it belongs.

   For example, if we find a leaf with a pinnate vein pattern, we know that that plant continues its life cycle through seed production in flowers.

2. Plants continue their life cycle in different ways. Botanists classify plants according to those methods of reproduction.

 Materials Needed

1. Colored chalks.
2. Double-stick masking tape.
3. Two copies of the paper samples (pages 26–30), cut into individual leaves and plants.

   Photocopy each set in a different color, or put a conspicuous dot on each sample of one set. This will make it easier for you to know which team has placed a sample on the blackboard, and also to redistribute the samples for a new game. Use a laminating machine or clear contact paper to protect the samples for repeated use.
4. A copy of the labels (pages 31–33).
5. A copy of the Teacher's Chart (page 36).

For each child

6. Copies of the "Plants" data sheets (pages 34–35). Tape the two sheets together so that the children can easily refer to them during the game. For the simple game, you may wish to block out unused portions of the data sheets.

 Getting Started

Note: The diagram of the plant world on the Teacher's Chart is in no way complete. I have chosen to include only those classifications which are more familiar and thus more meaningful to my students.

For the first few times a class plays, choose the simple format. I always start with the set of angiosperm plants, the subsets of dicots and monocots, and the subsets of palmate and pinnate leaves within the dicot subset.

1. Tell the children that they are going to play a game with samples of leaves and plants. They will play in two teams, and they will take turns sticking samples in the right place on the board. The object of the game is for their team to be the first to place all their plants in the proper subsets.

2. For you, the object is to teach classification and plant properties by having the class play this game several times. It is not necessary for the children to have a great deal of prior knowledge for success with this game. However, you may wish to review the children's knowledge of Venn diagrams and their experience with classifying leaves (Leaf Tic Tac Toe, page 13, and Inside Leaf Patterns, page 15).

 Procedure

Preparing the Game:

1. Divide the class into two teams according to seating, so it is easy to know whose turn is coming up.

2. Place a stack of samples on each side of the board. Each team uses its own stack.

    For the simple game, you may wish to use only the samples that belong to the diagrams you have selected.

3. Draw the Venn diagram outlines on the blackboard, using different colors for each subset. Make sure that you draw each

set and subset large enough for the children to place samples inside.

4. Place a label for each set and subset in its correct place on the board. For the simple game, the name should face out.

5. Place one sample from each team's stack in the same correct subset, so the children do not have to begin the game by merely guessing.

6. Emphasize that no comments are to be made during the game. Anyone who does so forfeits a turn for his or her team.

7. You may want to impose a time limit on each turn.

Playing the Simple Game

8. The first child on one team selects a sample from the team's stack and places it on the board. **Note:** If you use all of the samples, many of them will not belong to the diagrams you have selected. The children should therefore place these samples outside all of the sets. For example, if you are using a Venn diagram which has subsets drawn only for angiosperms, a child who selects a needle-leafed gymnosperm should place it outside the set of all angiosperms.

    If the placement is correct, you say "Yes." Then the next member of the same team comes up and places the next sample.

    If the placement is incorrect, you simply say "No." Then the child replaces the sample in the stack, and the first member of the other team selects a sample.

    The game continues the same way. The placing of samples shifts from one team to the other only when there is an error.

9. The simple game ends when one team properly places its last sample. That team is the winner.

Playing the More Complex Game

After your class has played the simple game several times, you are ready to present a more complex version to reinforce the names of the divisions of the plant kingdom. The children's object now is for their team to be the first not only to place all their plants in the proper subsets but also to correctly name each set and subset.

10. Draw the entire Venn diagram on the board. Then place the labels with the names turned toward the board.

    Follow instruction 8 above (ignoring the Note). Then:

11. When one team has correctly placed all of its samples, the next child up on that team has the job of naming the label for a set or subset.

    If the name is correct, turn the label over. Then the next member of the team gets to name another label.

    If the child misnamed the label, it is the other team's turn to continue placing samples or begin naming labels.

12. The first team to correctly name the last label wins the game.

13. After the first time your class plays the complex game, as all the labels are visible on the blackboard, you may wish to have the children fill in their Plant Chart. They can then use the chart as a reference during future games, and gain valuable experience reading Venn diagrams.

Strategic Tips

1. This game is wonderful for increasing observation abilities, and you will see a transfer of those skills into other curriculum areas.

2. Emphasize that scientists can and should learn from mistakes. Thus the children, as young scientists, can learn from mistakes made in the game. For example, if a child places a sample incorrectly, other team members now know where *not* to place the sample when it is their turn.

3. This game will help launch an understanding of how plants function and interact in ecological systems. To strengthen that awareness, use Woods Systems Sleuth (page 40) as a followup.

Dicot Pinnate-veined Leaves

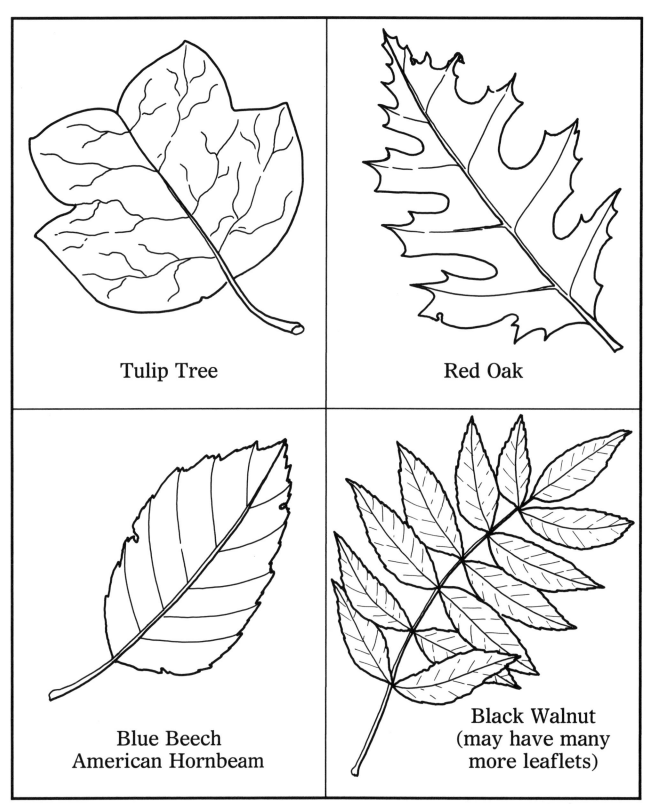

Tulip Tree

Red Oak

Blue Beech
American Hornbeam

Black Walnut
(may have many
more leaflets)

Dicot Palmate-veined Leaves

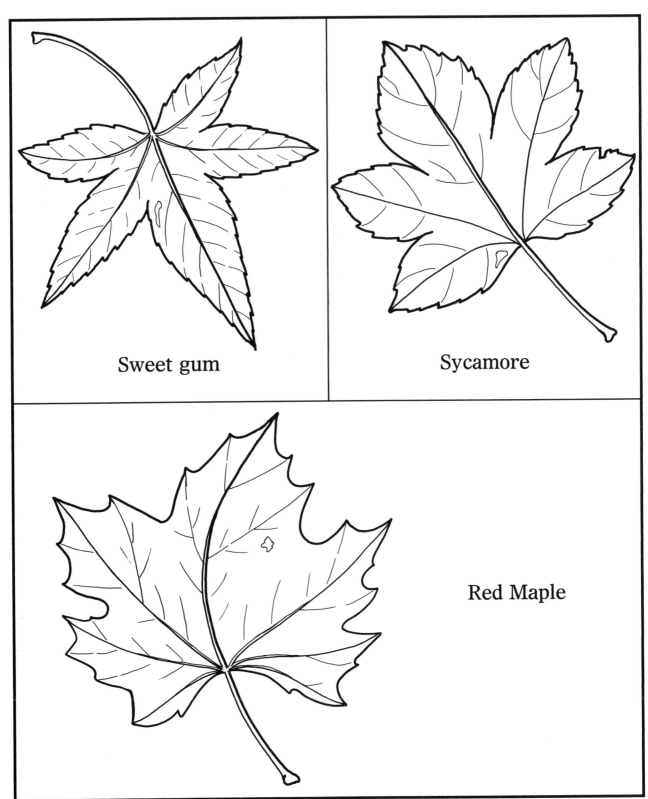

Sweet gum

Sycamore

Red Maple

Monocots
Parallel-veined Leaves

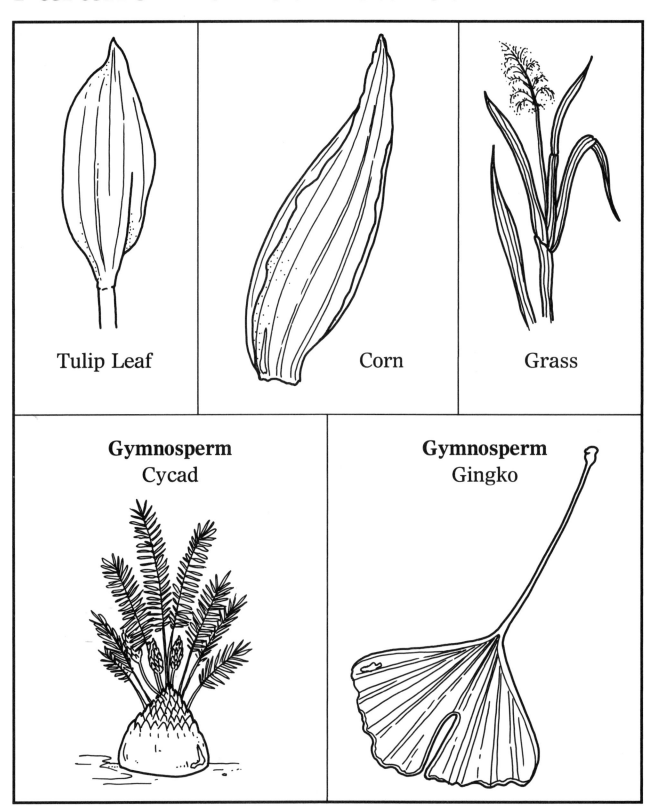

Tulip Leaf

Corn

Grass

Gymnosperm
Cycad

Gymnosperm
Gingko

Conifers (Gymnosperm)

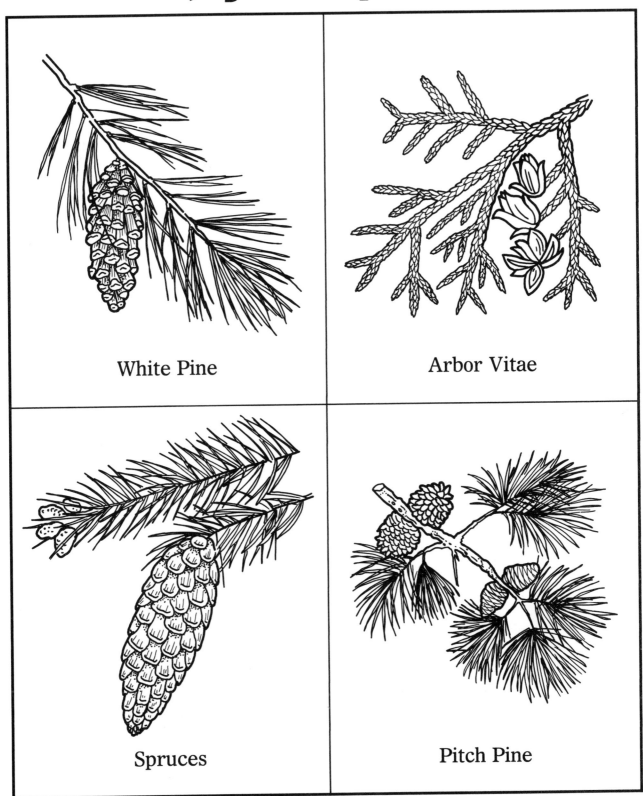

White Pine

Arbor Vitae

Spruces

Pitch Pine

Some Non-Seed Plants

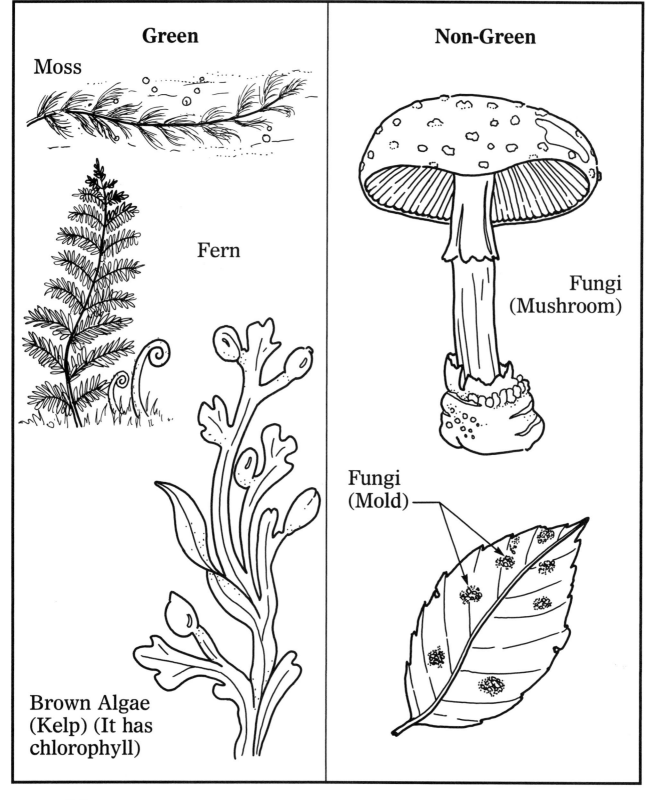

Green

Non-Green

Moss

Fern

Brown Algae
(Kelp) (It has
chlorophyll)

Fungi
(Mushroom)

Fungi
(Mold)

Angiosperm

Monocots

Dicots

Pinnate

Palmate

SEED PLANTS

Gymnosperm

Gingko

Conifers

Cycads

NON-SEED PLANTS

Green— Algae, Ferns
Mosses

Non-green— fungii, molds
(decomposers)

PLA

NTS

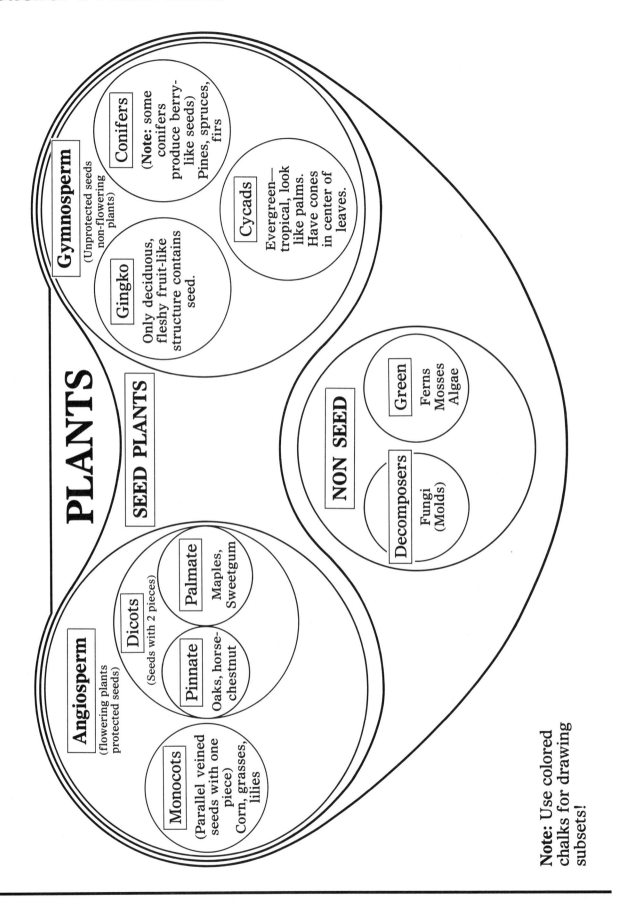

PLANTS

SEED PLANTS

Gymnosperm
(Unprotected seeds non-flowering plants)

Conifers
(**Note:** some conifers produce berry-like seeds) Pines, spruces, firs

Cycads
Evergreen—tropical, look like palms. Have cones in center of leaves.

Gingko
Only deciduous, fleshy fruit-like structure contains seed.

Angiosperm
(flowering plants protected seeds)

Dicots
(Seeds with 2 pieces)

Palmate
Maples, Sweetgum

Pinnate
Oaks, horse-chestnut

Monocots
(Parallel veined seeds with one piece) Corn, grasses, lilies

NON SEED

Green
Ferns Mosses Algae

Decomposers
Fungi (Molds)

Note: Use colored chalks for drawing subsets!

Overhead and Underfoot Walk
Woods Systems Sleuth

life

Overhead and Underfoot Walk is *recommended for Grades K–2*

Woods Systems Sleuth is *recommended for Grades 3–4 or as a followup to the above activity*

 Lesson Overview

A walk through a wood, or even a stand of trees on a playground, will challenge children to develop their skills of observation and (for the followup activity) inference. It will also enable them to discover these . . .

 Science Principles

1. A forest has distinct layers, and each layer has environmental conditions which determine the type of plant and animal populations found there.
2. Living and nonliving things interact to form systems in a forest. These interactions affect the members of the systems.

 Materials Needed

1. Colored chalk.

For each child

2. A pencil.
3. A clipboard (or piece of hard cardboard with paper clip).
4. Data sheet.

 Getting Started

Note: If you are using Woods System Sleuth as a followup, review the key points of this section only to the extent you consider necessary.

1. Use colored chalks to sketch a simple drawing of a forest scene on your board.
2. Ask the children if anyone has a canopy bed at home. Elicit that a *canopy* is like an umbrella that goes over your head.
3. Have the children look at the forest scene on the board, and ask them where the canopy would be. Inform them that the forest canopy can also be called the *overstory*.
4. Try to elicit where the *understory* and *ground level* of the forest would be.
5. With very young children, you might have them pantomime where each part of the forest is, and have them relate it to a part of their body.
6. Explain to the children that they are going to take a detective walk to discover what living things are found in each part of the forest. Before going out, they will make some predictions of what they might find in each layer.

 Procedure

Note: All of these steps apply to Overhead and Underfoot Walk. Those marked * also apply to Woods Systems Sleuth.

*1. You might have the children work as cooperative teams to discuss their predictions.
2. If your children cannot read, cue them to the correct boxes by means of the small squares

in the prediction boxes and small stars in the recording boxes. Older children should label their sketches.

*3. Discuss with the children what they should look and listen for in each layer of the woods. (See Background Information below.)

*4. Brief the children on the rules for behavior in the woods.

 Background Information

Sections marked * apply to Woods Systems Sleuth.

1. The *canopy* may contain birds' nests and squirrels' nests. A squirrel's nest is usually larger than a bird's nest, and is often leafy and rather sloppy looking.

   *Mention that squirrels assist in the dispersal of seeds, thus helping the continuation of a tree's life cycle while they enjoy the forest's food supply.

   *Birds which eat berries also help continue the plants' life cycle, as the seeds pass through their digestive systems unharmed and are dropped in other areas of the woods.

2. The *understory*, which is the tree trunk region, may reveal fungi, vines, insects, spiders and their webs, and woodpeckers.

   Shelf fungus and other varieties of fungus can be observed upon trunks and branches. Have the children notice whether the fungus is growing on healthy or dying trees.

   *Vines form a system with trees. The vines use the trees to reach the sunlight that the canopy shades out on the ground.

   *Small holes made by insects and woodpeckers are signs of systems between plants and animals. The children should be able to construct a food chain based upon this kind of evidence.

   *Larger holes can serve as homes to mammals such as raccoons or bats. (Do not permit children to place hands inside holes.)

   *Orb spider webs are evidence of interactions between trees, spiders, and insects.

3. The *ground level* may have many or few plants.

   *The canopy affects and is affected by the ground level. Dense shade from a very leafy canopy will encourage the growth of mosses and ferns. The decomposition of dead leaves will enrich the top soil, recycling nutrients needed by tree seedlings and other plants.

   Look for mushrooms, especially after a rainy period. (Caution the children against tasting any mushrooms.) Examine fallen leaves for other kinds of fungi: molds.

   *Molds help to decompose the dead leaves for recycling of nutrients.

   Have the children use twigs to scratch the top layer of soil to find earthworms. Observe whether the earthworms stay exposed or reburrow under the soil.

   *Earthworms help decompose the dead leaves to enrich the soil.

   Have children turn over logs to observe the amazing variety of insects and other arthropods living in their own decomposing worlds. (Also have them replace the logs with care.)

   Look for patches of greenish or gray lichen growing on rocks.

   *Lichen is a unique system of a fungus and algae interacting to benefit each other. The fungus acts as a sponge, absorbing water for both plants. The green algae perform photosynthesis, making food for both.

Overhead and Underfoot Woods Walk

l i f e

	■ I predict I will find:	★ I found:
Overstory (Canopy)	■	★
Understory	■	★
Ground Level	■	★

Woods Systems Sleuth

l i f e

How good a detective are you? How many systems or relationships (things that work together) can you find in the woods environment? Tell what and where.

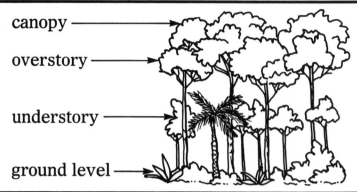

canopy ———
overstory ———
understory ———
ground level ———

System	What	Where I saw it
Plant and Plant		
Plant and Animal		
Animal and Animal		

Squirmy Science
Worm Motel (followup)

Both recommended for Grades K–4

Lesson Overview

A one-session investigation of earthworm behavior and physical properties is followed by longer-term observation, helping children to understand these . . .

Science Principles

1. Living things interact with and change the environment they live in.
2. Living things have unique properties (adaptations) which enable them to survive and to change their environment.
3. Worms are valuable members of their community (group of plants and animals) and ecosystem.

Materials Needed

1. A full sheet of black construction paper.
2. A clear tennis ball can with label removed, and half filled with layers (from bottom to top) of soil, sand, small pebbles, leaves, and grass. Sprinkle some water on top. Punch some holes in the lid for air circulation.

For each group
3. An earthworm.
4. A centimeter ruler.
5. Three paper plates.
   Plate 1 should have coarse sandpaper glued over half its area, with no gaps where a worm could crawl underneath.

Plate 2 should have a wet paper towel placed securely over half the area.
   Plate 3 has nothing on it.
6. A 4 × 4-inch sheet of black construction paper.

For each child
7. Data sheet and followup sheet.

Getting Started

1. Before the day of the activity, tell the children that they are going to study a wild animal in class. You may build up the suspense, or have them try to find out the animal by means of 20 Questions, before revealing that it is an earthworm. (It's useful to remind children that an animal does not necessarily have four legs and that a wild animal is not necessarily ferocious.)
2. Before class, prepare the plates for each group. Also prepare the tennis ball can "worm motel," since this will provide a storage place for the worms in Squirmy Science.
   Gather worms by assigning eager students either to dig in the soil outside the school or to bring worms from home in a covered container with soil, leaves, and a little moisture.

Procedure

1. Divide the class into groups and distribute the group materials and data sheets.
2. Tell the children that each group will investigate the preferences

of its worm by placing it first on Plate 1, then on Plate 2, and last on Plate 3, on which they will place the construction paper folded into a tent.

3. Ask the children to predict how they think their subject worm will react. Will it prefer a smooth surface to a gritty one? Will it prefer dampness to dryness? Will it prefer to stay in darkness or move into the light?

   Have them indicate their predictions on the data sheet by placing a P near each environmental condition they choose.

   Also have them give reasons for their predictions.

4. Have the children gently stretch out their worm and measure its length.

5. Now have the children gently run their fingers along the worm's skin and elicit descriptions of its segments, bristles, and muscular movements.

   Older children might briefly write up their descriptions. Younger children might imitate the worm's method of locomotion.

6. Now have the children in each group take turns placing the worm in the middle of each "environmental" plate. Each child should have two turns at each plate, so that the worm has eight choices for each environment.

   Each time the worm moves to one side of a plate, every child in the group places a tally mark in the appropriate box of his/her data sheet.

7. After the testing is completed, have each group place its worm in the "worm motel" for safety.

8. Gather data from each group to find out the classwide preferences of the worms. Note the results on the board with tally marks, and have the children note the classwide conclusions on their data sheet. Stress the importance of gathering large amounts of data to come to a valid conclusion.

9. Have the children hypothesize reasons for the worms' preferences.

10. Refer back to the children's first observations. Ask: *What are the bristles on the worms' bodies used for?* (To help the worms grip the soil as they burrow through it.) *Why don't worms have eyes?* (They live in darkness, but have light-sensitive spots on each segment.) *What are the rings on a worm's body?* (They are circular muscles that work with long muscles for locomotion.)

Worm Motel

 Procedure

1. Have the children draw their "before" observation of the layers of the motel.

2. Ask if there is anything else you can do to make the worms more comfortable in their motel rooms. The children should be able to tell you that the worms preferred to remain in the dark, so perhaps you should wrap some black construction paper around the motel.

3. Place the motel in a protected area in the classroom, where it will not be heated by the sun or a radiator.

4. Have the children observe the changes made to the layers over a period of days. They should then complete their data sheets.

   The children should conclude that the earthworm's burrowing behavior benefits the soil by making holes which permit air and water to circulate to plants' roots more easily. The worms also help to mix the soil layers.

Biologist _____

l i f e

Squirmy Science

▲ **PROBLEM:** Which conditions do worms like best?

   a. moisture or dryness
   b. rough or smooth surfaces
   c. darkness or bright light

■ **HYPOTHESES:** _____

● **METHOD:**

1. Place worm in center of moist/dry and rough/smooth plate. Tally each time worm moves to either side. Repeat 8 times.

👁 **OBSERVATIONS:**

1. Put tally marks in correct boxes.

Moist	Dry

Rough	Smooth

2. Place tent over worm. Time for 1 minute. How long did it stay in? Repeat 8 times.

2. The worm stayed in the tent:

_____ _____ seconds

_____ _____ seconds

_____ _____ seconds

_____ _____ seconds

★ **CONCLUSION:** Worms like _____

_____

Worm Motel

▲ **PROBLEM:** Can worms change their environment?

■ **PREDICTION:** _____

● **METHOD:**

1. Build worm motel.

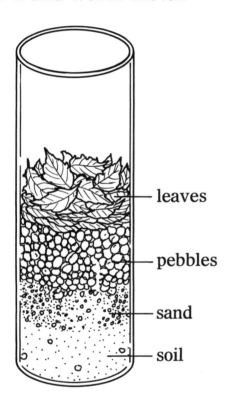

- leaves
- pebbles
- sand
- soil

2. Put worms in motel. Cover with black paper. Wait several days. Uncover and draw how worm motel looks now.

👁 **OBSERVATION:**

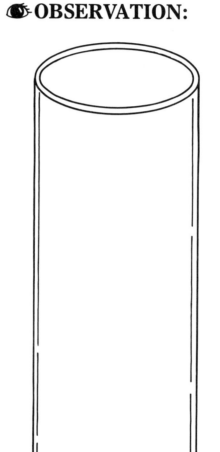

★ **CONCLUSION:** Worms _____ change their environment.

Worms can help the Earth by: _____

String Toss: A Mini-Ecology Study

l i f e

String Toss: A Mini Ecology Study *is recommended for Grades 2–4. May be adapted for Grades K–2*

Lesson Overview

One or two sessions centered on observing and comparing physical conditions and life forms in different outdoor environments, plus a followup assignment based on research and imagination, will lead your children to discover these . . .

Science Principles

1. An ecological *population* refers to the number of living things of one kind in an area. For example, the total number of ants in the area would be the ant population. Several populations coexist within one area.
2. An ecological *community* is composed of plants and animals living and depending upon one another in the same area.
3. The physical factors (environmental conditions) of an area will determine the variety of plant and animal populations in that area.
4. Environmental conditions affect the lives of plants and animals.
5. Plants and animals affect the environmental conditions.

Materials Needed

1. Three or four plant cuttings or potted plants. (Choose samples that would exist in the same physical area; in other words, do not mix cacti with broadleaf plants.)
2. One or two examples of a physical factor, such as a cutout sun and clouds or a few dead leaves (leaf litter).

For each group

3. A length of yarn tied at the ends to form a loop that will enclose an area the size you wish your children to study. (I usually have three meters of string for a group of four "ecologists.")
4. A centimeter ruler.

For each child

5. Data sheet and (if you plan to use it) followup sheet.

Getting Started

Note: Prior to this lesson your children should have played Ring Around the Plant World (page 23) so that they are familiar with the groupings of seed plants and non-seed plants, broad-leafed and needle-leafed plants.

1. Before class, select a variety of environmental areas, as close to the school building as convenient. You could include paved areas with weeds growing in cracks.
2. Seat the children in the groups in which they will be working cooperatively when they go outside.
3. Draw a chalkboard sample of the String Toss data sheet.
4. Inform the children that they will be going outside to study environments around the school,

and to find out if the types of plants in those environments are the same or different.

Each group will be responsible for studying an area that falls within a tossed loop of string. Each child will note information upon his/her data sheet, and will compare notes with the rest of the group later in class.

5. Ask the children if they would expect to find the same kinds of plants or animals living in the deserts of the southwestern United States as in the rain forests of South America.

6. Show your plant samples and ask each group to write a cooperative description of one plant. Have a member of each group read its description aloud, and then choose one description to model on the chalkboard data sheet.

Emphasize that knowing the names of the plants they will describe is not necessary.

7. Explain that *population* refers to the numbers of a specific type of plant, not to the total number of different plants.

Children need not attempt to count the populations of such plants as grass or moss. Older children can describe the fraction of the string-toss area which is covered by the plant, while younger ones can use such words as "most."

8. Show your cutout sun and clouds and/or dead leaves, and review environmental factors (amounts of sunlight, rainfall, and leaf litter, and type of soil). Ask what kinds of environmental factors the sample plant written about was living in. Remind the children to look for adaptations as clues, and to cite these adaptations in their answers.

9. Show the children the proper places to note environmental factors on the data sheet.

Discuss how to measure environmental factors. For sunlight, an estimate from none to plenty, based on the amount of shade and your local climate. For rainfall, a similar estimate based either on rainfall statistics or on the dampness of the soil. For leaf litter, the height of the pile of leaves in centimeters. For soil type, a range from pale and hard to dark and crumbly.

Procedure

1. When you arrive at the chosen environmental areas, either place each group's loop of string on the ground or have the children choose their own area.

2. Briefly review the key points of the investigation method.

3. The time needed for the outdoor activity is probably no longer than 30 minutes.

4. Allow classroom time after the activity for for the group members to share their information. Then have each group present its findings.

5. The class should be able to come to the conclusion that shady and sunny areas tend to support different populations of plants.

They should also be able to generalize from this experience to the conclusion that different environmental conditions will also affect the animal populations.

String Toss: A Mini-Ecology Study!

l i f e

1. Toss your string around an area and describe the following physical factors:

Amount of Sun	Amount of Moisture	Leaf Litter

2. Now describe at least 3 plants in your area using botanical vocabulary. Give the population of each plant species.

Description of Plants	Population

l i f e

Eat Your Way Through Botany
Professor __'s Great Botanical Discovery and How Do Seeds Travel? (followups)

All recommended for Grades 2–4

 Lesson Overview

In this multi-session mini-unit, the children will munch and crunch their way through the major parts of different plants. As they record their observations of edible roots, stems, leaves, flowers, and fruits, they will create their own reference guide and discover these . . .

 Science Principles

1. The parts of plants have specific functions which help them survive and continue their life cycle.
2. The parts of plants work together in a system.
3. Certain parts of plants interact with the environment.

 Materials Needed

For all sessions
1. Some small potted plants—one for the class and, if possible, enough for each student to take care of one. (You can create these plants inexpensively by taking cuttings from a few larger plants.)

For each group
2. One paper plate or napkin.
3. A container of water.

For each child
4. A copy of each page of the Eat Your Way Through Botany booklet (pages 55–58).

   Copy pages 1 and 4 of the book-let on the reverse side of pages 2 and 3, and the author page and page 5 on the reverse side of the title page and page 6. You can then fold the sheets together to form the booklet.

5. The followup data sheets (if you plan to use them).
6. (Optional) A hand lens.

For Roots
1. One well-established potted plant that can be lifted out of the pot with its ball of soil attached. (Test this in advance!)
2. One round slice of peeled carrot for each child, and one larger un-peeled section for each group.

For Stems
1. One inch-long section of celery stalk for each child, plus two or three whole stalks of celery with leaves attached for the class.
2. Food coloring.

For Leaves
1. One small piece of lettuce (pre-ferably not iceberg) for each child, plus one whole head for the class.

For Flowers
1. One very small floret of broccoli for each child.
2. For each group, one live cut flower which has a highly visible stamen and an abundance of pol-len, such as a tiger lily.

For Fruits/Seeds
1. Two bowls or plastic containers, quart size or larger.
2. One plastic knife for each group.
3. One small paper cup and a spoon for each child.

4. A different fruit for each group. I suggest cucumber, zucchini, squash, tomato, banana, apple, orange, strawberries.

5. One or two fresh green peas for each child. (Each group could share the peas from one pod.) If you can't get peas, unshelled peanuts are fine.

6. Enough dried peas or beans (such as limas or lentils) for each group or child to plant three.

7. Enough small plant pots for the planting. Or you can use styrofoam cups, which are reusable. (Paper cups molder.)

8. Potting soil for the planting.

Session One: The Roots

 Getting Started

1. Before class, place at least one potted plant on each group's table. If you have several different plants, place a variety on each table.

2. You can open the lesson by writing this rather corny statement on the board: *I'm "rooting" for you to have a great time in science today!* Challenge the children to come up with the subject to be discussed.

3. Have the children draw or write a description of one of the potted plants. Challenge them to make the description so complete and accurate that their neighbor can figure out which plant it is. Allow time for sharing descriptions and guesses.

4. Point out that everyone described leaves and other visible parts, but there are very important parts that normally cannot be seen. Elicit that these parts are the roots. Ask: *What good are the roots if you can't even see them?*

5. Call up a few volunteer "hurricanes" to blow on the plant as hard as they can. Before they blow, ask the children to predict what will happen to the plant.

   Of course, they will not be able to dislodge the plant from the pot. Ask the children what this experiment reveals about one job of the roots. (Anchorage.)

6. Ask if the children know any other jobs performed by the roots. Some will probably know that roots absorb water. Reinforce this knowledge by permitting the children to water the plants at this point.

7. Hold up the large, well-established plant whose roots you have tested in advance. Announce that you are going to pull the plant out of its pot, and ask the children to predict what will happen to the soil. (Most will delightedly predict a big mess on the floor.)

   Gently pull the plant out by grasping the stem so that the soil comes along bound to the roots. The children will be amazed and thus receptive to the idea that roots prevent erosion of soil.

   If you live near a sandy beach or an area that is dusty in dry weather, ask the children what happens when they go there on a windy day. Most will recall getting sand or dust in their eyes. Link that to the relative lack of plants in the area. Point out the importance of grasses in preventing further erosion of beaches or soil.

 Procedure

1. Place the plates of sliced carrots and the section of unpeeled carrot on each group's table.

2. Allow the children time to observe the carrot slice (with hand lens, if available) and to sketch it in the space provided in the botany booklet.

3. Have them observe the unpeeled carrot and note the fine extensions (root hairs). Explain that when a carrot is pulled up, most of its root system is left behind. Ask the children what they think the root hairs do in the soil. (Absorb water and minerals.)

4. Tell the children they are going to discover another important job of a root by eating a carrot slice very slowly. They are then going to vote on the most noticeable taste by choosing from the following: sweet, bitter, salty, and sour. Allow voting for two or more tastes.

5. Tabulate the results on the board. The vote should reflect sweetness and, possibly, bitterness.

6. Have each group read the cloze story of the roots (page 1 of the booklet) and allow time for them to write answers. Acceptable answers might be: 1. absorb or drink; 2. hold or anchor; 3. sugar; 4. soil; 5. system or team.

7. End this session by allowing the children time to reflect on the mystery: *Where does the root get its sugar?*

Session Two: The Stem

Note: This session requires a brief followup one or two days later. (See Procedure step 6.)

Getting Started

1. Ask the children what would happen to leaves if there were no tree trunks. (The leaves would all be close together on the ground and thus receive less sunlight.) Show a potted plant and ask what part does the same job as the trunk and branches of a tree. (The stem.) Elicit that one job of a stem is to support leaves.

Procedure

1. Place the plates of celery pieces on each group's table.

2. Tell the children that they will be allowed to "play" with their food today, but first they must sketch their piece of celery on page 2 of the booklet.

3. Show the celery stalk with leaves and ask if anyone knows what plant part you eat when you crunch on celery. If necessary, point to the stem of a potted plant again.

4. Encourage the children to notice the strings in their celery pieces and the openings in the strings at the cut ends. Have them try to peel off some strings and then squeeze the piece to see if anything comes out of the openings. (Water.) Elicit the hypothesis that strings carry water from the roots to the leaves. (You might also wish to introduce the word *xylem* for the string-like tubes.)

5. Try the old experiment of placing a few celery stalks in water with food coloring added. Ask the children to predict what might happen, and also how long it will take to happen. Make a written note of the predictions.

6. Wait a day or two to allow the children to observe that the xylem has transported the colored water to the leaves. Then have them complete the cloze statements on page 2 of the booklet. Acceptable answers: 1. leaves; 2. stem; 3. xylem; 4. roots.

Session Three: The Leaf

 Getting Started

1. Remind the children of the mystery of the carrot's sweetness (The Roots, step 7 of Procedure). Tell them that today they will finally solve it.

2. Ask for a really brave volunteer. Inform her that she will have to say goodbye to her family for two weeks and stand in a bucket of soil. She will be placed in the sun, given fresh air, and watered. But she will not be given any food.

   (If anyone objects that she cannot absorb water because she has no root hairs on their feet, tell them she will be allowed to drink water.)

   Ask the children to predict what condition the child will be in after two weeks.

3. At this point pretend to notice that there is something wrong with the child: she is not green. No matter how smart she is, she couldn't learn to do what a green plant can do to survive.

   Point out that your plants are green and have gotten bigger over the past two weeks. Yet all you gave them was fresh air, water, and sunlight—no food. Where did the food come from?

4. Encourage the children to recall the sweetness of the carrot roots, and elicit that the sweetness has to be sugar.

   Tell them that a special "factory" in green plants can rearrange carbon dioxide (from the air) and water to produce sugar. To do this the factory must have a green chemical called chlorophyll, which can take energy from sunlight to "cook" the ingredients.

Ask what part of a plant is green and is exposed to air, water, and sunlight, and the children will deduce that the leaf is the sugar factory. (With older children, you may wish to mention that the name of this food-making process is *photosynthesis*, in which *photo* refers to light and *synthesis* to making or putting together.)

 Procedure

1. Place the plates of lettuce pieces on each group's table.

2. Have the children observe the leaves and draw them, including the veins for carrying water and sugar. If your children have done the Inside Leaf Patterns activity (page 17 or 18), have them classify a whole lettuce leaf as well.

3. Have the children eat the lettuce. Ask if it is very sweet, and the opinion most likely will be no. Ask where the sugar went. Elicit that some was used for growth and the remainder was sent down to the roots for storage. (You might add that the tubes which carry the sugar down are called *phloem*.)

4. To discover why plants need to store food, have the children think of times when a leaf wouldn't be able to make sugar, such as at night or on very cloudy days. Mention that deciduous trees also use stored sugar in early spring, when they have no leaves and need food to grow new ones.

5. Elicit the fact that roots and leaves form a system, since the roots provide the leaves with water to help make sugar, and the leaves send sugar to the roots for storage.

6. Have the children complete the cloze sentences on page 3 of the

booklet. Acceptable answers:
1. sugar or food; 2. air or carbon dioxide, water, chlorophyll, and sunlight or energy; 3. sugar, cloudy or dark, spring.

Session Four: The Flower

 Getting Started

1. Have a brainstorming session with the children on what flowers make them think of. Ask why so many flowers are attractive in both color and scent. Establish the fact that some flowers are even more attractive to insects or birds than to people.

 Procedure

1. Distribute a flower to each group. Have the children place their fingers on the stamen's anther to simulate a bee visiting the flower. Their fingers should be able to pick up some pollen, just as the bee's hairy legs would. Have the children transfer the pollen to the center of the flower. Then have one child from each group transfer pollen to the flower of another group. Based on their experience, children should now give a definition of *pollination.*

2. Have the children sketch the flower in the space on page 4 of the booklet. (Make sure they leave room for a later sketch of broccoli.)

3. Ask if any children suffer from hay fever. What makes them sneeze? Point out that very small flowers, and many odorless flowers, have their pollen spread by the wind. Also, while many flowers have to receive pollen from a different plant, some can be *self-pollinated.* This means that pollen may simply fall from the anther into the same flower.

4. Distribute the plates of broccoli. Have the children examine the small flower buds and sketch them in their booklet.
   Check for understanding of pollen distribution by asking how broccoli is likely to be pollinated. (Wind and/or self-pollination is the logical answer.)

5. The children may now eat their (broccoli) flowers. Afterward, have them take a closer look at their larger flowers. Elicit that a bee would go for nectar deep inside the flower. Have the children locate the pistil (it is usually slightly swollen and centered within the petals). Point out that if pollen gets knocked off the bee's legs (children's fingers) it will most likely land on the pistil.

6. Announce that the pistil has something inside it very much like what chickens lay. The children may be astounded that flowers contain eggs (ovules), and astounded again when you tell them that pollen grains contain sperm. When pollen lands on the pistil, the pollen grain grows a tube, and the sperm travels through it to reach the ovule.

7. Some children will probably know that when sperm enters an egg an embryo is created. Ask what kind of baby would be created in a plant. Elicit the response of *seed* by asking what you plant to get new plants.

8. Have the children complete the cloze sentences in their booklets. Acceptable answers: 1. life cycle; 2. eggs or ovules; 3. pollen or sperm; 4. pistil; 5. seed or embryo.

Session Five:
Fruit and Seeds

 Getting Started

1. Tell the children that they are going to make a salad today. (Avoid using the word *fruit* until Procedure step 3.)

 Procedure

1. Hand each group a plate with a different fruit and a plastic knife. Have one child slice the "food" with the knife.

2. Ask each group to give a complete description of what they observed both on the outside and on the inside of the food.

   Elicit that all of the objects had seeds either in or on them. Were all the seeds edible?

3. Combine the banana, apple, orange, strawberries (and/or other sweet fruits) to create a salad, and ask what kind it is. (Fruit salad.) Remind the children that all of these fruits had seeds in them.

4. Combine the cucumber, zucchini, squash, tomato, etc., and ask if anyone knows what kind of salad is in this bowl. Prompt the children by asking if these ingredients also have seeds. Elicit that these items are also fruits, because they contain seeds.

   I always make a joke about supermarkets mislabeling these food items as vegetables. Have the children brainstorm other fruits commonly called vegetables.

5. Have the children taste both kinds of fruit salads, and encourage comments.

   Ask if they have ever eaten watermelon and spat the pits onto grass. Ask what would happen if the pits (seeds) were left undisturbed.

6. Have they ever seen birds eating berries and creating a mess? What are the birds helping to do after they eat? (Caution the children that some berries which are safe for birds are poisonous for humans.) After a horse eats an apple whole, what happens to the seeds?

7. Help the children realize that many plants' life cycles depend upon the spreading of seeds by animals. The tastiness of many fruits is nature's way of making sure that the seeds are dispersed. This is an example of plants and animals helping each other.

8. Ask the children how seeds that are not edible might be spread. At this point you need not elicit all possible ways. Discuss one major way, such as the wind. In fact, you might elicit this method by having the children recall how pollen is spread.

9. Have the children complete the cloze on page 5 of the booklet. Also encourage them to illustrate the page with cross-sections of fruits. (I challenge them to draw at least five fruits of different colors.)

   Acceptable cloze answers: 1. seeds; 2. anything edible with seeds inside or outside; 3. flower; 4. pollination.

10. Distribute the pea pods or peanuts. Have the children open the pods/shells and try to peel off the outer seed coats. They should then be able to split the peas/nuts in half.

    Have them examine the inside (with hand lens, if available). Guide them to observe the small seed leaf, and ask if anyone knows what this is. (A baby plant.)

11. Have the children cooperatively complete the cloze on seeds. Acceptable answers: 1. plants; 2. life cycle; 3. pollen grains or sperm, egg or ovule; 4. animals, wind (or whatever method was discussed in step 8).

12. Have each child or group plant three dried peas or beans in a small cup of potting soil. Assign the children to keep a diary on the development of their plants.

Professor ____'s Great Botanical Discovery

 Procedure

1. Distribute the data sheets and review the contents.
2. Tell the children that they may invent a plant, but it should be like a real plant, with roots, stem, leaves, flowers, fruit, and seeds.
3. The completed sheets might form a bulletin board display.

Travels With a Seed

 Procedure

Note: If all the seed types on the data sheet are not found in your locality, you may wish to tape replacements over them, or delete them, before copying.

1. Tell the children that they will be going outside to look for different ways of traveling. No, not cars or planes or boats, but ways that seeds travel.
2. Distribute the data sheets and discuss the different kinds of seeds. Draw examples on the board or show pictures.

   Explain that *samaras* are seeds with wings, like maple or tulip tree seeds; *acorns* travel with an-

imals; *hitchhikers* have pointed spikes that cling to fur (or clothes); and dandelions and cottonwood have seeds with *parachutes*.

3. Have the children work in groups, perhaps with each child responsible for one type of seed. Lead the children to a suitable area with trees and wild flowers.
4. Afterward, have each group share its findings with the class.

Eat Your Way
Through Botany

By Botanist

_____

1. Seeds have baby _____ inside them.

2. Seeds help the plant complete the pattern of its _____.

3. Seeds are made by _____.

4. Seeds travel with _____ or _____.

6

About the Author

_____'s favorite edible
fruits and vegetables are:

1. Fruits have _____ inside.

2. Some edible fruits are: _____
   _____

3. All fruits come from the pistil of a
   _____.

4. Fruits form after bees or wind cause
   _____.

1. A flower's job is to help the plant complete its _____.

2. The pistil has _____.

3. The stamen makes _____.

4. Animals or wind help pollen travel to the _____.

5. This makes a _____.

1. Roots _____ water.

2. They _____ the plant in soil.

3. They contain _____.

4. Roots help Earth by holding the _____ together.

5. Roots and the Earth are a _____ that works together.

1. Stems raise _____ to reach the sunlight.

2. A tree's trunk is a _____.

3. Water travels through tubes called _____.

4. Xylem carries water from the _____ to the leaves.

2

1. Leaves make _____.

2. Leaves need _____, _____, and _____ for photosynthesis.

3. They send extra _____ to the root bank for _____ days, and early _____ when the tiny new leaves (buds) can't make food.

3

Great Botanical Discovery (followup)

l i f e

1. Draw the stages of a plant's life cycle you have discovered.
2. Use the 2 lines to explain how its seeds are spread. You may illustrate it, too.

seed
soil

soil

soil

soil

seed
soil

Travels With a Seed

l i f e

1. Draw the seed in each box below.	**2.** Explain how it should travel in each box below.	**3.** How many?
samara		I found
acorn (nut)		I found
hitch-hiker		I found
parachute		I found

Word Box

squirrel	travel	buries
wind	blow	fur

Edible Plant Venn Diagram Game

Recommended for Grades 2–4. Can be adapted for Grades K–1

Lesson Overview

This lesson should be preceded by Eat Your Way Through Botany (page 48) to ensure that children are familiar with plant parts and functions.

In this game the children try to identify the edible parts of various fruits and vegetables. As they sharpen their observation and classification skills, the children also review these . . .

Science Principles

1. Each part of a plant has a particular function in the system of the plant as a whole.
2. Parts of many plants are edible, and in some cases edibility helps the part to perform its function.

Materials Needed

1. One copy of the illustrations and labels on pages 63–67.

    Shade the copies of the illustrations with appropriate crayon colors. Laminate the copies, or cover them with clear contact paper, and then cut out the individual illustrations and labels.

    Note: If the classification of potato as a stem is likely to confuse your students, you may wish to substitute an edible stem that is more familiar to them (e.g.

bamboo shoots, sugar cane, rhubarb, asparagus).
2. Double-stick masking tape.

Getting Started

1. Draw the Venn diagram outlines (pages 68, 69) on the board, making sure they are within the children's reach. Place the appropriate part label within each ring, but do not place function labels at this time.
2. Tell the children that they are going to play a team game with "food."

Procedure

1. Divide the class into several cooperative teams.
2. Tell the children that you will give a picture of a fruit or vegetable to each team in turn. The team is to agree on which part of the fruit or vegetable is edible. One child from the team will then use masking tape to place the picture in the diagram ring on the board.
3. You may wish to impose a time limit on each turn.
4. Select a picture and hold it up. The team that is "it" brainstorms and tries to place the picture correctly. Depending on the placement, you simply say "Yes" or "No."
5. If the placement is correct, the same team continues with the next picture you select. If the placement is incorrect, the next

team tries to place the same picture.

6. *For the simplified version of the game* (with younger children), the team which correctly places the last picture is the winner. You may then review the functions of each plant part as you place the function labels on the board. *For the full version*, follow steps 7–9 instead.

7. When all the pictures have been used up, tell the children that the game is not over. The team that is "it" now has to choose a plant part and describe its function.

8. If the description is correct, you place the function label in the appropriate ring. If the description is incorrect, the next team chooses a part and describes its function. (If only one function is left, the team must of course choose that.)

9. The team which correctly explains the last plant part function wins the game.

 Strategic Tips

1. Be sure to emphasize that in this game the children should classify plants according to the part that is most edible or most commonly eaten. For example, classify corn as seed because cobs are not eaten; broccoli as flower because only part of the stem is eaten; tomatoes, bananas, squash, strawberries, etc., as fruit even though they contain seeds, since they are eaten for their flesh.

2. Emphasize that teams can benefit from other teams' mistakes, since they will know what placement or explanation is *not* correct.

3. Encourage the children to review their Eat Your Way Through Botany booklets both before the game and during any breaks.

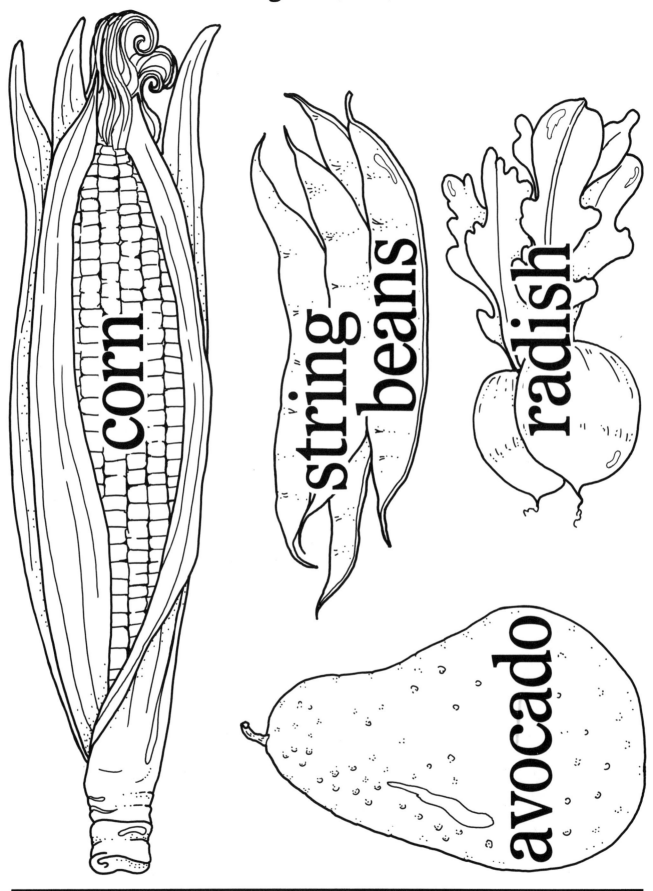

corn

string beans

radish

avocado

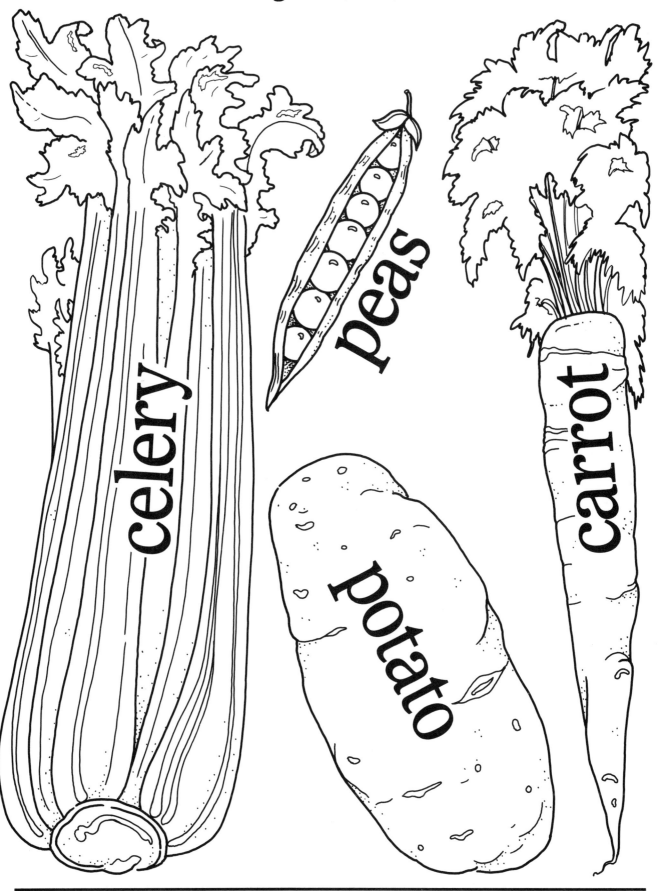

celery

peas

potato

carrot

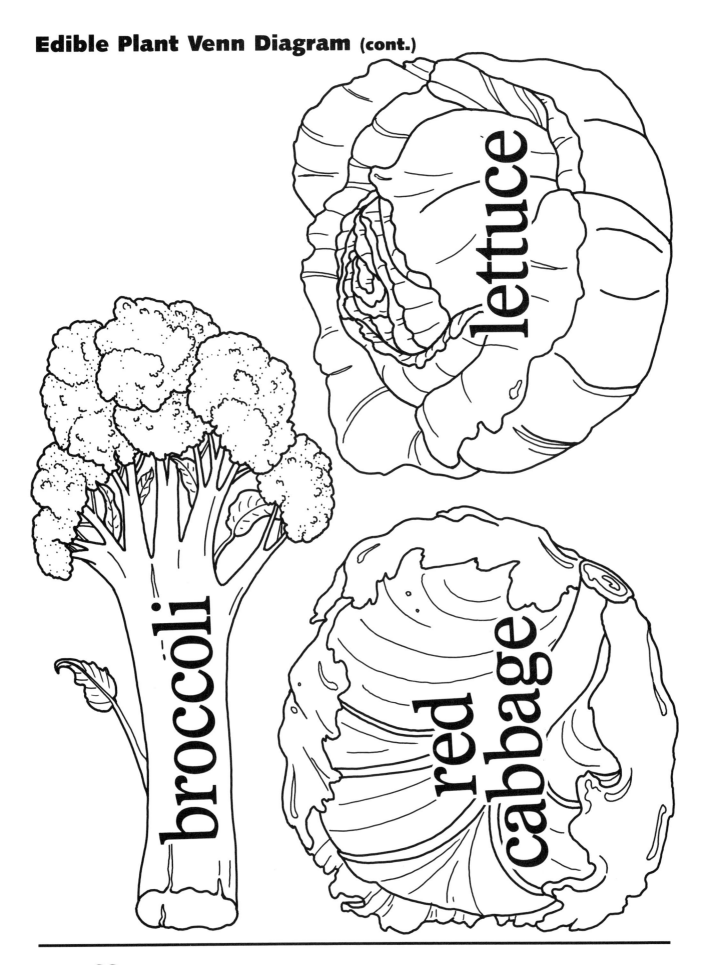

Part labels

VEGETABLES

FRUITS

Seeds

Stems

Leaves

Flowers

Function labels

Seeds—continue life cycle

Stems—support plant; transfer water

Leaves—produce sugar out of water and carbon dioxide.

Flowers—produce seeds when pollen enters ovule. (Pollination)

Fruits—hold and spread seeds

Teacher's Guide: Edible Plant Venn Diagram
(Simpler, lower grade version)

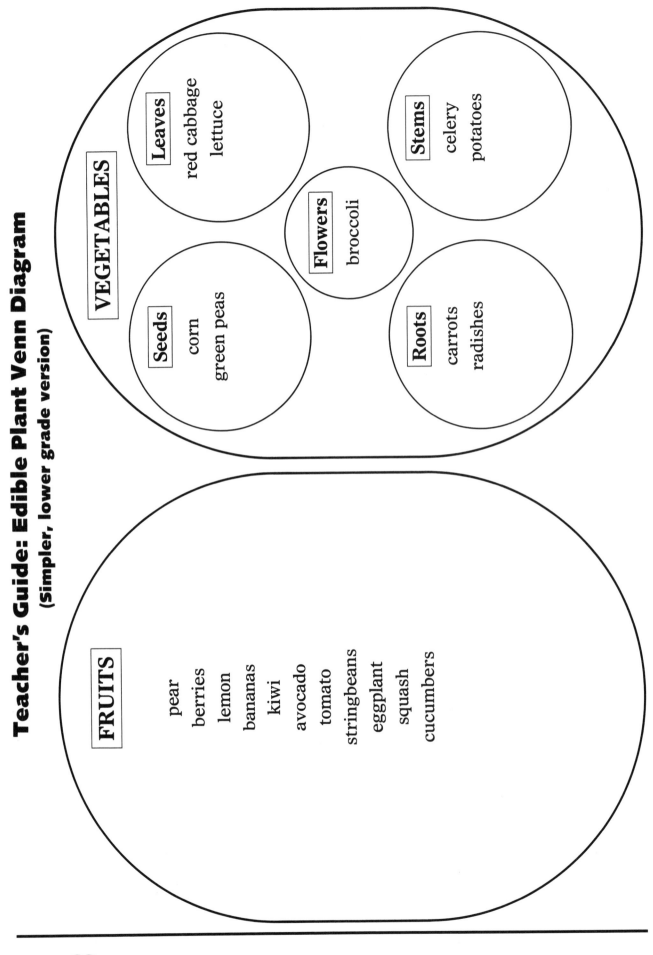

VEGETABLES

Leaves
red cabbage
lettuce

Stems
celery
potatoes

Flowers
broccoli

Seeds
corn
green peas

Roots
carrots
radishes

FRUITS

pear
berries
lemon
bananas
kiwi
avocado
tomato
stringbeans
eggplant
squash
cucumbers

Teacher's Guide: Edible Plant Venn Diagram
(Upper grades or Experienced Players)

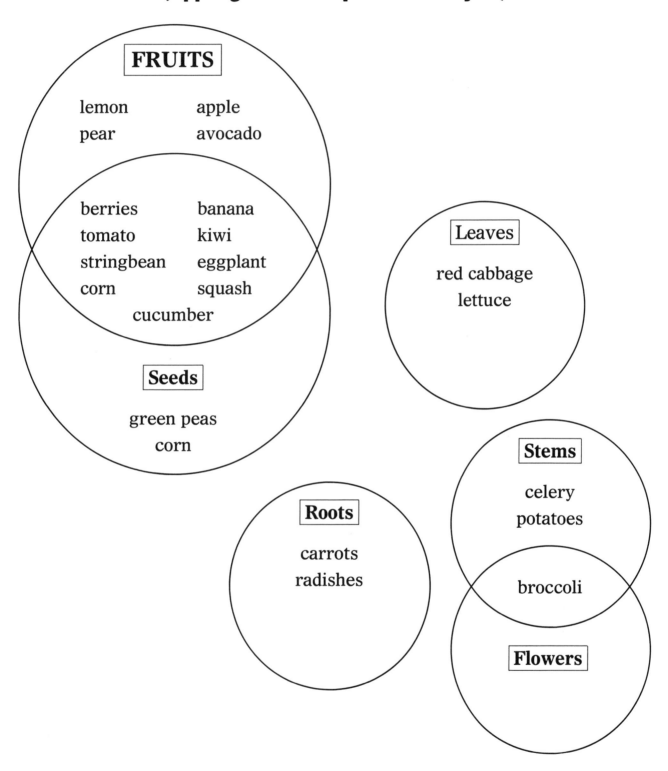

FRUITS

lemon   apple
pear   avocado

berries   banana
tomato   kiwi
stringbean   eggplant
corn   squash
cucumber

Seeds

green peas
corn

Leaves

red cabbage
lettuce

Roots

carrots
radishes

Stems

celery
potatoes

broccoli

Flowers

Please note: Corn is included in the intersection of fruit and seed, because the definition of grain is a seed and fruit. However, some books show corn to be classified as a seed. Hence, either placement should be considered correct by the teacher.

l i f e

Lunchbox of Nutrients
Read The Label (Consumer Science homework followup)

Lunchbox of Nutrients *is recommended for Grades 2–4*

Read the Label *is recommended for Grades 3–4*

 Lesson Overview

Simple testing for nutrients in seeds, using iodine and brown paper, will allow student chemists to discover these . . .

 Science Principles

1. Seeds have properties that allow the embryo inside to grow and develop into a new plant, thus continuing the plant's life cycle.
2. The nutrients which enable the embryo to survive also make seeds a nutritious part of our diet and the diet of many animals.

 Materials Needed

1. A small, untippable container of iodine with medicine dropper (for your use only).
2. One bottle of corn oil.
3. One slice of bread.

For each child

4. One paper plate or towel.
5. One uncooked soaked lima bean. (Soak the beans overnight.)
6. One frozen or canned pea, corn kernel, and lima bean. (If frozen, the peas should be thawed overnight.)
7. A strip of brown kraft paper, about 1 × 4 inches. (You can cut

these out of brown paper bags. Keep an extra strip for yourself.)

8. Data sheet and (if used) followup sheet.

 Getting Started

1. Write "Lunchbox of Nutrients" on the chalkboard. If any children ask what this means, tell them they will find out during the lesson.
2. Inform the children that they are going to perform a "dissection" to find out if it is really true that seeds have baby plants inside them.

 Procedure

1. Pass out one soaked lima bean and paper plate or towel to each "surgeon."
2. Have the children carefully remove the outer seed coat and then open the bean into two halves.

   You may wish to point out that the lima bean is a *dicot seed*, which means it is easily split into two parts. A seed such a corn kernel is *monocot*, which means it has one part and is not easily split in two.
3. Have the children observe the inside of the bean halves. They should then draw and label what they see in the "Sketch Box" on the data sheet.

   Lead the children to realize that there is a baby plant (embryo) packed into all the seeds.

4. Have children hypothesize about what else is packed into the seed. Prompt them with questions. Would the children use a green crayon to color the leaves in their sketch? (No, the leaves are not green and therefore do not have chlorophyll.) Would the leaves be able to get sunlight? (No, they are inside the seed.) So could these leaves make food by photosynthesis? (No.) Then how will the embryo grow to reach the sunlight?

   By this time someone should have hypothesized that the remainder of the material in the seed must be food for the baby plant.

5. Ask what kind of food the embryo would need. Elicit the word (or concept) *nutritious*—for example, by asking if the embryo would want junk food. Then point to the word *nutrients* on the board and ask if children know what these are. If necessary, define the word and then have the children brainstorm the kinds of nutrients they have heard of. (The major ones are *protein* for building muscles, simple or complex *carbohydrates* for energy, and *fats* for storage of energy.)

6. Inform the children that they will be performing tests on three kinds of seeds to determine if these contain two of the major nutrients—starch (complex carbohydrate) and oil (liquid fat). In other words, *Did the baby plant come packed in its own lunchbox?*

7. Distribute the peas, limas, and corn, and the brown paper strips.

8. Have the children fold the brown paper strip into thirds and label each section with the name of a different seed.

9. Demonstrate the test for oil by pouring a few drops of cooking oil on your brown paper and then holding it up to the light. The paper becomes translucent when fat (oil) is present. (Do not let the class see that the oil you are testing is corn oil.)

10. Have the children test their seeds by breaking them in half and rubbing the inside of each onto the appropriate section of the brown paper. As reinforcement of the difference between dicot and monocot seeds, the children will find that the monocot corn kernel does not readily split in half. They will probably have to squeeze the contents out of the seed coat.

    To avoid mistaking water for oil, give the brown paper time to dry. Tell the children not to write observations until after the next test.

11. To test for the presence of starch, iodine is used. It will turn black or purplish when in contact with starch. **CAUTION: Warn the children not to touch the iodine. It is poisonous if ingested and can stain clothing. Tell them that only you will be dispensing it.**

    Go around the class and place a drop of iodine on the inner portion of each of the three seeds of each child.

12. Have the children note whether the iodine changes color from its original rusty hue and enter observations 4, 5, and 6 on their data sheets. (All of the seeds should test positive for starch.) You might discuss which seed made the iodine change most dramatically, and what this means. (The seed contains more starch than the other seeds.)

13. Now have the children look at their oil test papers and note the data. (Only the corn should test positive for oil.)

14. Have the children construct their concluding statements by reviewing their observations. Make the children aware of the value of their note taking skills.

15. To check for understanding, hold up the bottle of corn oil and ask if anyone knows which seed it was made from—pea, bean, or corn.

Strategic Tips

1. With younger children, you might have them perform the same tests but not fill in individual data sheets. Instead, you could compile information on a classroom experience chart modeled on the data sheet.

2. In step 12, some children may jump the gun and note that starch is present in their observation recording spaces. This is a valuable error, since it allows you to point out the difference between an observation and an inference. The observation can only be what is observed by the senses—in this case, the color change.

3. The fact that each child does his/her own food testing reinforces the idea that experiments must be duplicated many times in order to reach a valid conclusion.

   Before the children write their conclusions, you might want to have them work in groups to pool their observations and reach a group conclusion.

4. As a followup, Read the Label (below) not only reinforces the nutritional information in Lunchbox of Nutrients but also makes children aware of the powerful information they can obtain from food labels.

Read the Label

 Procedure

1. Review the data sheet with the class. Be sure to ask if the serving sizes are the same in each of the three labels. Discuss why it is important to check this when comparing labeled foods.

2. If the children have not worked with food labels before, you may wish to discuss questions 1–4 in class. Encourage the children to give reasons for their answers.

Lunchbox of Nutrients!

l i f e

Draw and label the parts of your seed.

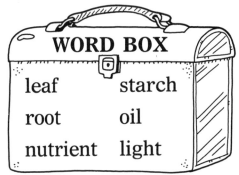

WORD BOX

leaf	starch
root	oil
nutrient	light

▲ **PROBLEM:** Do seeds have food?

■ **HYPOTHESIS:** I think seeds _____

_____

_____

● **METHOD:**

1. Rub bean on paper.

2. Rub pea on paper.

3. Rub corn on paper.

4. Put iodine on bean.

5. Put iodine on pea.

6. Put iodine on corn.

OBSERVATION:

1. _____

2. _____

3. _____

4. _____

5. _____

6. _____

★ **CONCLUSION:** I found out that seeds _____

_____

Seeds are _____ for people to eat.

Read the Label!

l i f e

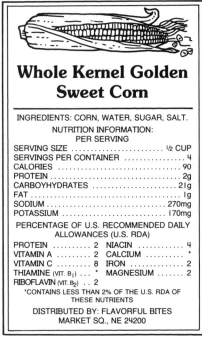

Whole Kernel Golden Sweet Corn

INGREDIENTS: CORN, WATER, SUGAR, SALT.

NUTRITION INFORMATION:
PER SERVING

SERVING SIZE	½ CUP
SERVINGS PER CONTAINER	4
CALORIES	90
PROTEIN	2g
CARBOHYDRATES	21g
FAT	1g
SODIUM	270mg
POTASSIUM	170mg

PERCENTAGE OF U.S. RECOMMENDED DAILY
ALLOWANCES (U.S. RDA)

PROTEIN	2	NIACIN	4
VITAMIN A	2	CALCIUM	*
VITAMIN C	8	IRON	2
THIAMINE (VIT. B₁)	*	MAGNESIUM	2
RIBOFLAVIN (VIT. B₂)	2		

*CONTAINS LESS THAN 2% OF THE U.S. RDA OF
THESE NUTRIENTS

DISTRIBUTED BY: FLAVORFUL BITES
MARKET SQ., NE 24200

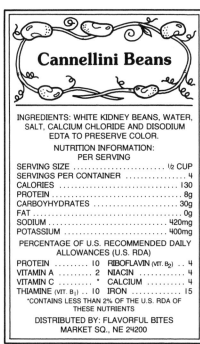

Cannellini Beans

INGREDIENTS: WHITE KIDNEY BEANS, WATER, SALT, CALCIUM CHLORIDE AND DISODIUM EDTA TO PRESERVE COLOR.

NUTRITION INFORMATION:
PER SERVING

SERVING SIZE	½ CUP
SERVINGS PER CONTAINER	4
CALORIES	130
PROTEIN	8g
CARBOHYDRATES	30g
FAT	0g
SODIUM	420mg
POTASSIUM	400mg

PERCENTAGE OF U.S. RECOMMENDED DAILY
ALLOWANCES (U.S. RDA)

PROTEIN	10	RIBOFLAVIN (VIT. B₂)	4
VITAMIN A	2	NIACIN	4
VITAMIN C	*	CALCIUM	4
THIAMINE (VIT. B₁)	10	IRON	15

*CONTAINS LESS THAN 2% OF THE U.S. RDA OF
THESE NUTRIENTS

DISTRIBUTED BY: FLAVORFUL BITES
MARKET SQ., NE 24200

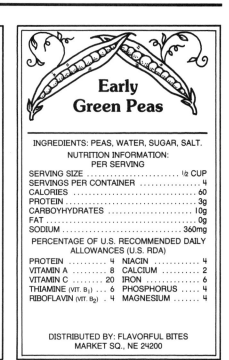

Early Green Peas

INGREDIENTS: PEAS, WATER, SUGAR, SALT.

NUTRITION INFORMATION:
PER SERVING

SERVING SIZE	½ CUP
SERVINGS PER CONTAINER	4
CALORIES	60
PROTEIN	3g
CARBOHYDRATES	10g
FAT	0g
SODIUM	360mg

PERCENTAGE OF U.S. RECOMMENDED DAILY
ALLOWANCES (U.S. RDA)

PROTEIN	4	NIACIN	4
VITAMIN A	8	CALCIUM	2
VITAMIN C	20	IRON	6
THIAMINE (VIT. B₁)	6	PHOSPHORUS	4
RIBOFLAVIN (VIT. B₂)	4	MAGNESIUM	4

DISTRIBUTED BY: FLAVORFUL BITES
MARKET SQ., NE 24200

1. Which seed is highest in:

fat? _____ starch (carbohydrates)?_____

2. Carbohydrates give you energy. Which seed would you eat if you were going to run a race and no other food was handy?

_____

3. Which seed has the most muscle building protein? _____

4. Overall, which seed is most nutritious? _____

5. On the back of this paper make a chart. Look at five foods at home, read their labels and fill in the chart. Here is a sample of how to do it:

Food	Carbohydates	Fat	Main Ingredients	From
Bread	13g	2g	Flour	Seeds

Be a Twig Surgeon

l i f e

Recommended for Grades 2–4. Can be adapted for younger children

Lesson Overview

You will need to introduce and set up this activity as part of one session and complete it in another session several days later.

The children will test the effect of removing leaves on a twig's ability to transpire water. The experiment will lead to these . . .

Science Principles

1. Living things have properties and behaviors that help them adapt to and survive in their environments.
2. The process of *transpiration* (loss of water through *stomata* or pores in a leaf) is necessary to regulate the amount of water present in a plant.
3. Forests contribute to the water cycle through the transpiration of water vapor into the atmosphere.
4. Most broadleaf trees lose their leaves in the fall to avoid the loss of irreplaceable water during winter, when ground water is frozen.

Materials Needed

1. Large container of water.

For each child

2. Two leafy twigs of the same variety and size.

3. Two glasses or beakers.
4. Two plastic bags large enough to enclose the twigs.
5. Tape, twist-ties, or rubber bands to close the bags.
6. Data sheet.

Getting Started

Note: With younger children, have them perform the experiment without using the data sheet. Omit step 2 below, and eliminate references to the data sheet in steps 2 and 6 of Procedure.

1. Show the children one of the twigs and ask what the leaves are doing. Someone should be able to tell you that they are breathing—taking in carbon dioxide and putting out oxygen. Ask if they can see the leaves doing anything else. Then tell them that they are going to perform an experiment to find out something else that the leaves are doing.
2. Distribute the data sheets and review the first section (on the definition of *transpire*). Caution the children to look for a dictionary definition which fits a botanical context. Then have them complete this section.

Procedure

1. Distribute the materials for the experiment.
2. Review the rest of the data sheet, making sure that the children understand what is required.
3. Have the children carry out Method step 1. Ask them to check that the bags are dry inside. End the first session here.

4. After several days, students should be able to observe water droplets forming in the bag with the leafy twig. There will be little if any water in the other bag.

5. Ask the children how the water got into the bag. Remind them that the bags were dry before they were sealed around the twigs. Elicit how xylem tubes transport water to the leaves. Remind the children that all the variables in the experiment have been kept the same—except for the presence of leaves in one bag.

6. The children should infer that leaves breathe out not only oxygen but also water vapor. Have them write their conclusions.

7. Ask if anyone knows why deciduous trees lose their leaves during the winter. (To avoid water loss.) Also elicit why evergreens don't lose their leaves. (Needle-leaf trees and cacti transpire very little because their leaves have a much smaller surface than those of deciduous plants. Other evergreens' leaves are coated with a waxy substance that prevents transpiration.)

8. Challenge the children to invent a way to keep their plants from drying out during vacation. (Bag the entire plant.)

Strategic Tips

1. You have set up a water cycle in the bags. Review evaporation, condensation, and precipitation.

Dr. _____

Be a Twig Surgeon

To be qualified to do your surgery, you must first write the definition of TRANSPIRE after you use the dictionary. Then use it in a sentence.

_____

_____

You know that leaves breathe in carbon dioxide, and breathe out oxygen helping animals with their breathing. BUT

▲ **PROBLEM:** What else does a leaf breathe out?

■ **HYPOTHESIS:** _____

● **METHOD:**

1. Find 2 leafy twigs. Remove all the leaves from 1 twig. Put a plastic bag over each twig. Wrap and tape the bags tightly to the stem of the twigs.

2. Place twigs in water and sunlight. Observe conditions in bag over a couple of days.

👁 **OBSERVATION:**

1. (This is what the experiment should look like.)

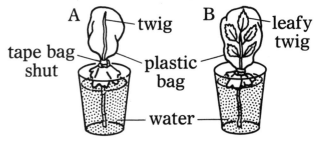

2. Bag A _____

   Bag B _____

★ **CONCLUSION:** Leaves breathe out _____ besides oxygen.

I know that because _____ .

Leaves transpire _____ .

_____

l i f e

The Food Chain Drama Game

Recommended for Grades K–4, depending on the vocabulary used

 Lesson Overview

In this game, children role-play the links in food webs and chains, and thus demonstrate these . . .

 Science Principles

1. Energy is never lost; it only changes its form.
2. Most food chains begin with green plants, which use solar energy to produce food. Therefore green plants are known as *producers.*
3. Animals may eat green plants and be *primary consumers,* or eat other animals and be *secondary consumers. Decomposers* such as bacteria and fungi serve as recyclers of nutrients and energy from dead members of food chains.
4. Food chains are linked together to form food webs.
5. A change in the population of plants or animals in a food chain will affect other members of the chain and its web.
6. Environmental conditions affect and are affected by food webs.

 Materials Needed

1. One copy of the food chain game cards (pages 80–85). Color them with appropriate crayons. Laminate the sheets, or cover them with clear contact paper, and then cut out the individual cards.

 Getting Started

1. Inform the class that they are going to be actors in a thrilling life and death drama.

 Procedure

1. Randomly distribute the cards face down to members of the class. Do not worry if there are not enough for everyone. Tell children who do not receive cards that they will function as directors of the dramatic "plays."
2. The children now look at their cards. Point out that each card has a symbol on it—a triangle, square, circle, or star.
3. When you call out a symbol, the "actors" with those cards are to come "onstage" to the front of the room and stand side by side holding up their cards.
4. Look at the lineup and say something like: *According to the way you are standing, the insects eat the toad, which eats the leaves, which eat the bacteria and fungi.* Ask the class: *Does this sequence make sense? Is there a director who can straighten out this play?*
5. One or more "directors" may help to untangle the food chain. The players then say their lines, such as:
    Player 1: I am the leaves (producer). I use (solar) energy from the sun to make (produce) my own food.
    Player 2: I am an insect. I eat (consume) the leaves for my energy.

Player 3: I am the toad. I eat (consume or prey upon) the insects for my energy.

Player 4: I am the bacteria or fungus. I decompose everything left over when it dies in this food chain. I recycle nutrients and minerals so more green plants can grow for other food chains.)

6. Ask what would happen if there was a drought and the plants in the area died. (The food chain would break.) What if insecticide killed insects, birds ate them, and then other animals ate the birds? (The insecticide poisons would affect other members of the chain.)

7. Repeat with other chains.

 Strategic Tips

1. Older children should be encouraged from the start to use scientific terminology (e.g. the parenthesized words in step 5). Even with younger children you can broaden the vocabulary after they have acted out several chains or played the game several times. For example, they can learn to use *herbivore* for plant eater, *carnivore* for animal eater, and *omnivore* for eater of both plants and animals.

2. Reverse the order in which the players speak. For example: I am an insect—I give energy to the toad because I am its prey.

3. Challenge more advanced students to create their own food chain game cards after selecting secondary consumers and researching back along the food chains. The cards should be the size of playing cards, illustrated and labeled, with each card in the same chain marked with the same symbol. The players take turns placing cards in rows on a desk.

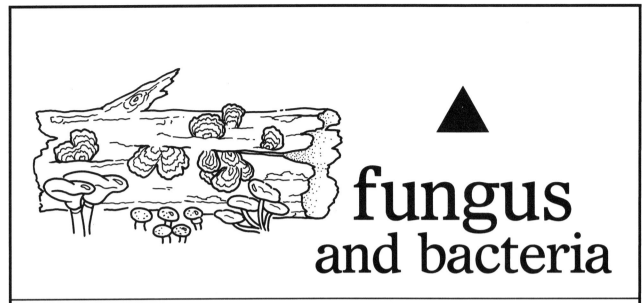

▲

fungus
and bacteria

▲

seeds

▲

mouse

★

fox

★

bacteria and
mushrooms

●

grass

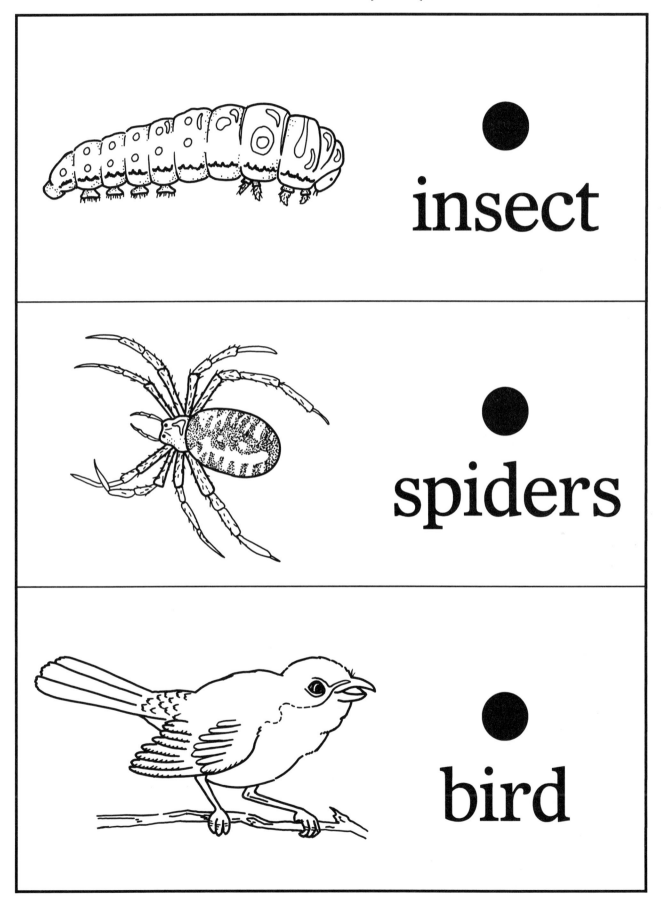

insect

spiders

bird

mushrooms
and bacteria

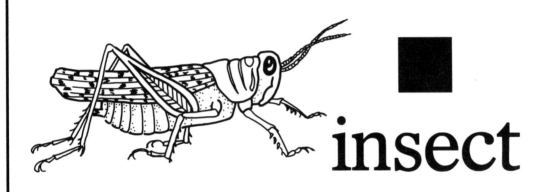

insect

leaves

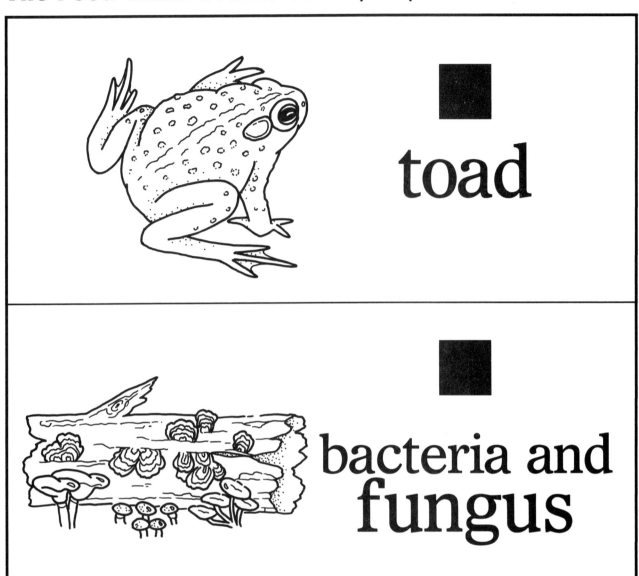

toad

bacteria and fungus

earth

Air: A Weighty Topic

Recommended for Grades K–4

 Lesson Overview

Observing, replicating, and inferring from simple hands-on experiments with plastic bags, bottles, and water will lead students to discover these . . .

 Science Principles

1. Air is all around us.
2. Two objects cannot occupy the same space at the same time.
3. Air is matter because it takes up room, and has mass (weight).
4. Air presses down.
5. Air is fluid and takes the shape of the container it is in.

 Materials Needed

1. A clear, empty squeeze bottle (e.g. a liquid soap refill.)
2. Several plastic bags of different shapes and sizes.
3. A clear plastic (watertight) shoebox or container deep enough to contain a plastic cup. One for each group of four students, if possible; otherwise one for the class.
4. One clear plastic cup per shoebox.
5. One or two paper towels per shoebox.
6. One 12-inch (30-cm) ruler for each group.
7. Two balloons of equal size.
8. Balance scale or wire hanger with thread to construct your own "dirt cheap" balance scale.

For each child
9. Data sheet.

 Getting Started

1. Before class, prepare the balance scale for weighing the balloons. Tie equal lengths of thread to each end of the hanger. Then tie the end of each thread around each tied off balloon end. To use the balance, raise it by placing a pencil under the hanger hook.

   Go around the room squeezing the "empty" bottle at all the students. They will squeal and jump as the air rushes out and tickles them.

   Ask: *Why are you laughing? I thought this bottle was empty. Did you see anything come out? Did you feel anything? Hear anything?* The children should be able to tell you that air was in the bottle.

   Establish the fact that air is "sneaky" and flows back into the bottle the second you stop squeezing it. (Air is fluid.)
2. Ask the children to predict what shape air will take if you pull a plastic bag through the air. (Air takes the shape of its container.)
3. Ask the children if there is air in their desk, or in a closet. Some may not be too sure. Pull a plastic bag through the closet or the inside of the desk to demonstrate that it can be filled with air. (Air is all around us.)

Procedure

1. To prove that air takes up room, you need the clear shoebox filled with water plus the cup and paper towel. Tell the children you are going to perform a "magic trick." Challenge them to watch closely and see if they can perform it as well.

2. Call up a student to verify that the paper towel is dry. Then crumple the paper towel and place it securely in the bottom of the cup.

    Ask for a prediction of what will happen to the paper towel if you place the cup into the water upside down.

3. Invert the cup and hold it straight down as you slowly submerge it in the water. Then pull it out of the water, still keeping it totally vertical.

    Remove the towel and have the student verify that it remained dry.

4. Ask why the paper towel stayed dry. Elicit that there was air taking up room in the cup along with the paper towel. The air prevented water from entering the cup, because two objects cannot be in the same place at the same time.

5. Ask the children to draw the experiment in the proper space on the data sheet. Older students should label their drawing and write a summary of the experiment.

6. Allow the groups to perform the "magic trick" (either with their group shoeboxes or by taking turns with the class box).

7. To show the effects of air pressure, place a ruler on the table so that about one third extends over the edge. Tap this end gently, and the ruler will fall off the table. Invite a student to do the same.

8. With the ruler in the same position on the table, place a data sheet over it. Invite the student to tap the ruler with the same degree of force as before. This time it will not fall!

9. Elicit that air was pressing on the larger surface of the paper and therefore on the ruler as well. This pressure was greater than on the ruler by itself.

10. To check for understanding, ask what would happen if a sheet of newspaper was placed upon the ruler. (It would be even more difficult to knock the ruler down, due to the increase in surface area and in the total amount of air pressure on the ruler.)

11. Allow each group to try the experiment. While students are awaiting their turn, they can sketch, label, or write a brief summary of the experiment in the appropriate place on the data sheet. (Air presses down.)

12. To demonstrate that air has weight, ask the children to predict which is heavier, an inflated balloon or an empty balloon. Many children will predict the empty balloon is heavier, because they associate filled balloons with "floatability" in the air.

13. Demonstrate that both empty balloons are the same weight on the balance scale.

14. Inflate one balloon. Place it and the uninflated balloon on either side of the balance. The balloon filled with air will make its side of the scale tip slightly lower.

15. Have the class complete the data sheet.

Air: A Weighty Topic

Draw a picture of the experiment that shows:
(Label it and explain it if you can.)

> Air takes up room.

_____

_____

_____

> Air presses down.

_____

_____

_____

> Air has weight.

_____

_____

_____

Air: It Matters To Us All!

Recommended for grades K–4

Note: This lesson can be used to teach fire safety concepts.

 Lesson Overview

Air is matter in a gaseous phase. Observations of simple but exciting teacher demonstrations with a balloon, an egg, and other common objects will lead children to realize these . . .

 Science Principles

1. Matter can be found on Earth in solid, liquid, and gaseous phases.
2. Air is a gas.
3. When air is heated, it rises.
4. Air is composed of different gases. (78% nitrogen, 21% oxygen, and 1% carbon dioxide and other gases.)
5. Air makes up our Earth's atmosphere (the gas surrounding a planet).
6. Air can be used to help us accomplish work.

 Materials Needed

1. A glass baby bottle or other bottle which can be subjected to heat.
2. 2 balloons with neck large enough to fit over the glass bottle.
3. A pan, basin or other heatable water container.
4. A hot plate or electric fry pan
5. Several paper towels.

6. An empty, clear 64 oz. apple juice container with a neck opening just large enough to support a hardboiled egg.
7. Matches
8. 2 peeled, hard-boiled eggs
9. Packing wrap with air bubbles
10. A data sheet for each student.

 Getting Started

1. I always begin this lesson by trying to walk through the door without opening it. (I get a big laugh when I pretend to bang my nose, and ask why couldn't I get through?
2. Discuss that fact that any material (matter) that takes up room and space is made of small building blocks called molecules. The analogy to blocks allows the children to visualize the idea that molecules can be arranged in different ways to create many kinds of structures. Molecules are like Legos that are too small to be seen.
3. Next, I usually announce that I am going to stand on the air. (I step off a chair and, of course, end up on the floor.)

    This leads to the question, *How do molecules arranged in a solid door compare to molecules arranged in the air?*

    The children infer that solids have molecules packed closely, and air molecules are very far apart.

    Introduce the word *gas* to describe molecules which are very far apart.

Procedure

1. Call up three to five children (depending on available space). First have them simulate molecules in the door by joining hands and standing close together, so that they stop you when you try to walk through. Then have them drop hands and move apart to simulate air molecules. Now it is easy to weave your way through them.

   Other groups of children may repeat this simulation.

2. Ask the children to use dots to draw molecules in a solid and a gas in the spaces provided on the data sheet. Ask them to infer how molecules would be arranged in a liquid, and then draw them. (Not as close together as in a solid and not as far apart as in a gas.)

3. Elicit what would happen if a bunch of molecules had to stand on a hot plate. Would they stand still, or would they tend to jump around in a hot-footed dance?

4. Show the children the heat-resistant bottle with the balloon stretched over its opening. Establish the fact that there are air molecules in the bottle.

5. Place the bottle in a hot water bath on the hot plate, and ask for predictions about what will happen to the balloon as the air molecules get heated.

   The balloon will rise as the air molecules gain heat energy, collide with each other, and spread apart, increasing the empty space between them and thereby decreasing their density. The only place the molecules can go is up into the balloon.

   Ask: *What will happen when the sun causes air to warm?* (The air will rise.) *Will other air move in to take its place?* (Yes.) This moving air is what we call wind.

6. See if anyone can explain why fire safety rules call for crawling out of smoke filled rooms. (Smoke, which is hot air filled with the particles of combustion, rises, leaving a cooler, safer section of air near the floor.)

7. Ask the children to complete the box which best fits the above demonstration: Hot air rises.

8. To demonstrate that air is made of different gases, one of which is oxygen, and that fires require oxygen, and to reinforce the fact that air pressure pushes down, announce to the children that they are about to see the most amazing feat you have ever performed.

9. Crumple some paper towel and place it inside the apple juice bottle. Light a match and toss it inside the bottle. Let the fire catch. Place the peeled, hard-boiled egg upon the bottle opening and watch as . . .

   Hot air inside the bottle rises and escapes, making the egg wobble a little. The egg will appear to be sucked into the bottle, in one piece. This may happen quickly or slowly, depending upon how much hot air escaped.

   Elicit that the reason the egg fell into the bottle is that there was less air (and pressure) inside the bottle than before the fire, and the greater pressure outside pushed the egg in.

10. After the applause, the children will beg you to do the "trick" again. When you try it, you will have no success getting the fire to start inside the bottle. This will prove that an important part of the air (oxygen) was used up by the previous fire.

11. To demonstrate that air can help us do work, first show the

children a book and a balloon and challenge them to find a way a way of raising the book using the balloon. Give them time to brainstorm. (Place the uninflated balloon under the book, with the opening of the balloon accessible to your lips. Blow air into the balloon, and the book will rise.)

Ask if anyone can think of forms of transportation which use air in the same way. (Tires on cars, bicycles, etc.)

12. Show the children the plastic bubble wrap and ask them to explain how it protects packed objects.

13. Allow time for completing the final section of the data sheet (Air can help us do work).

 Strategic Tips

1. It is crucial to establish the concept that there are empty spaces between molecules. This will allow you to introduce the concept of the water cycle and the following three lessons entitled "The System We Live On—Planet Earth."

Air: It Matters to Us All!

e a r t h

Matter is made of molecules that can be close together or further apart. Draw a model of the molecules in a:

Solid

Gas

[ ]   [ ]

Door

Air

Think

How would molecules be arranged in liquids?

[ ]

Draw a picture of the experiments that show:
(Label it and explain it if you can.)

Hot air rises.

Air is made of different gasses.

_____

_____

_____

_____

Air can help us do work.

_____

_____

The System We Live On—Planet Earth!

Part One: Can Soil (a Solid) Hold Air (a Gas)?

e a r t h

Recommended for Grades K–4

 Lesson Overview

Students will discover that mixing soil and water not only makes mud-pies but also stirs up these . . .

 Science Principles

1. Two objects cannot occupy the same place at the same time.
2. Two or more objects that interact are called a system.
3. Matter is changed during interactions within a system.
4. The size and shape of particles will affect the way they fit together and help determine the amount of space between them.
5. The solid, liquid, and gaseous phases of matter determine the behavior of the matter.

 Materials Needed

1. A globe.
2. A small piece of scrap paper.

For each group

3. One clear plastic cup (5 ounce).
4. Enough soil to fill each cup one-third high.
5. A container of water (about half a litre or one pint).
6. One 30 ml measuring cup (easily found in over-the-counter children's medicines—parents are a good source of these).

For each child

7. Data sheet.

 Getting Started

1. Before class, test the amount of water needed for the soil as described in Procedure step 5.
2. Ask if anyone knows what system we live on. Someone may chime, "The Solar System," but the real answer is that we live on the system called planet Earth.
3. Challenge the children with the following riddle: *Why is the Earth like a loaf of bread?* Show the globe, and ask if anyone knows the answer to the riddle. Explain that the Earth's outer covering is called the *crust*, just like the outer covering of bread. The crust is composed of solid land masses, with large expanses of liquid water separating them.
4. Ask: *Does anyone know the name for all the air which surrounds the Earth?* The word *atmosphere* really means air around a ball (or any rounded object, such as a planet).
5. Tell the children that today they are going to do an experiment to see how a liquid, solid, and some gases of the Earth act as a system.

   To be sure that children understand what a system is, brainstorm some examples of systems (e.g. a tree, an automobile, a sports team) and then ask for a definition: A system occurs when two or more objects work together. The children should also understand that systems can be human-made or natural.

Procedure

1. Have the children observe the cups of soil, and ask each group for a description. Be sure that the word *particle* is mentioned. Ask if the particles fit precisely together like building blocks, or if there may be spaces between them.

2. Ask if anyone thinks there might possibly be air in the spaces inside the soil. In other words, can soil (a solid) hold a gas (air)?

3. Before proceeding to the method, invite a student up to the front of the room to stand on a tiny piece of paper. Tell the class that it is the "Special Spot." Invite another student up to stand on the whole "Special Spot" at the same time as the first student. This, of course, is impossible. Elicit that the only way both students can stand on the entire spot is to take turns or push each other off.

4. This will pave the way for understanding that if water is poured into the cup of soil, and if there is already air in the spaces between the soil particles, the water will push the air out. Therefore bubbles of air will rise to the surface.

5. Invite the children to proceed with the method and observation described on the data sheet.

   The observation of bubbles will depend upon the quality of your soil, so experiment with it beforehand to establish the quantity of water necessary to push air bubbles out. In general, I have found that 30 ml of water poured into a 5 ounce cup filled about halfway up is sufficient.

6. Before the children proceed to the conclusion, you may wish to ask if living things are found in soil. Elicit the fact that animals and plants can survive in soil be-

cause air is present.

Invite your groups to brainstorm what animals depend upon air sneaking its way into the soil.

Ask if anyone has ever noticed what worms do right after a heavy rain. (They come to the surface, because the heavy soaking drives their air supply out.)

Besides worms, insects, moles, rabbits, and other burrowing animals depend on air in the soil. The roots of plants need air surrounding them, as well.

Acceptable cloze answers: 1. air; 2. system; 3. animals survive in the soil.

Strategic Tips

1. When the students are recording their observations, be sure they understand that they cannot see the air, but only the bubbles. The conclusion is the proper place to infer that air was in the bubbles.

2. The word *system* is a great beginning for a word map, for which the children brainstorm different types of systems—both natural and human-made. The organization of the word map can also show connections, grouping some systems as subsets of other systems. This would make a good homework assignment for grades 3 or 4.

The System We Live On—Planet Earth!

e a r t h

1. The Earth's crust is made of liquids, solids and gases.

2. How do they work together in a system?

▲ **PROBLEM:** Can soil (a solid) hold air (a gas)?

■ **HYPOTHESIS:** _____

● **METHOD:**

1. Look at and feel the soil.

2. Measure 30 ml of water. Pour it into the soil.

👁 **OBSERVATION:**

1. The soil _____

_____

2. When the water goes into the

soil, _____ come

out. The soil _____.

★ **CONCLUSION:**

1. The water pushed _____ out of the spaces between the soil particles.

2. The soil and air are a _____.

3. They help _____.

The System We Live On—Planet Earth!
Part Two: Can Water (a Liquid) Hold Air (a Gas)?

Recommended for Grades K–4

Lesson Overview

A transparent glass of water allows children to discover why marine life can exist, along with these other . . .

Science Principles

1. Liquid matter is made of molecules with empty spaces between them, allowing other molecules to fill in those spaces.

   (See other science principles listed in the previous lesson.)

Materials Needed

1. A clear plastic cup filled with marbles.
2. A clear, slightly smaller plastic cup containing sand. Determine exactly how much sand the cup of marbles can accommodate and place that amount in this cup.

For each group
3. A plastic spoon.
4. A clear plastic cup (any size).
5. Freshly drawn tap water.

For each child
6. Data sheet.

Getting Started

1. Announce that you are going to pour the sand into the marble cup. Ask for a prediction of what will happen. (They will gleefully predict a mess of sand on the floor.)

   The children will not realize how much empty space there is between the marbles.
2. Now pour the sand. Explain that the marbles represented molecules, and the sand was able to fit into the spaces between the molecules.

Procedure

1. Have the children focus on the question on the data sheet: *Can water hold air?* In other words, can a liquid hold a gas?

   Encourage discussion by providing hints such as: *Have any of you had any soda lately?* Also remind the children that all living things need air to survive.
2. Have the children place the spoon in the transparent cup of water, and watch. Within several minutes they will see very small bubbles appear on the spoon.

   The written observation should mention bubbles, not air—which has the property of being invisible.
3. The conclusion should reflect the awareness that air is present in water, and should lead to a discussion of marine life depending upon the dissolved oxygen in water.

   Acceptable cloze answers to worksheet questions: 1. bubbles, air; 2. system; 3. fish (or other marine life); 4. algae (seaweed), etc.

The System We Live On—Planet Earth! 2

▲ **PROBLEM:** Can water (liquid) hold air (gas)?

■ **HYPOTHESIS:** _____

● **METHOD:**

Place spoon or object in cup of water. Wait and watch.

👁 **OBSERVATION:**

_____

_____

_____

★ **CONCLUSION:**

1. I saw _____ form in the cup. This proved that

   _____ was in the water.

2. A liquid and gas worked together to form a _____.

3. Air in water helps animals like _____

   _____ survive under water.

4. Plants like _____ can also survive under water because of this system.

The System We Live On—Planet Earth!
Part Three: Can Molecules Jump?
Puddle Jumpers (followup)

Both recommended for Grades K–4

 Lesson Overview

A molecular race, painting with water, and observing the effects of heat and wind lead children to these . . .

 Science Principles

1. Molecules which absorb energy move more rapidly.
2. Rapidly moving surface molecules will escape from water to become vapor or steam in the air.
3. The more surface area exposed, the greater the evaporation rate of water.

 Materials Needed

1. (Optional) A hot plate with a beaker of boiling water.
2. A small lamp with its shade removed.
3. A globe.

For each group

4. A centimeter ruler.
5. Two 30 ml measuring cups.
6. Two paintbrushes.
7. A sheet of 8 × 11 paper folded into a fan.
8. A small plate or tray.

For each child

9. Data sheet and followup sheet.

 Getting Started

1. Refresh the children's memory of the dancing hot-footed air molecules in the hot air balloon experiment (page 92). Elicit that air molecules rise when heated due to their "stepped up" activity.

2. Ask if anyone thinks it possible for other molecules besides air to do some jumping. Provide a hint by asking if anyone has ever seen water boiling. Ask for a description of the bubbling appearance. (If possible, have a hot plate in your room, with a beaker of boiling water evident.)

   Announce that today the class will test water molecules to see if it's possible to get them to do some jumping without boiling the water. Allow time for your groups to hypothesize cooperatively.

 Procedure

1. Explain that each group will paint two 10 × 10 cm squares of water on a table top. At the same time, you will paint a 10 × 10 cm square of water on the board. At your signal, one square on the table will be fanned vigorously, and the other square will be left alone. You will hold the light bulb near the board, utilizing the heat to try to get the water to disappear.

2. Before starting the activity, discuss the fact that models are used in science to provide simulations of reality.

Elicit that the fanning represents wind energy (energy of movement) and the light bulb represents solar energy.

Explain that the square of water which is being left alone is called the *control* in the experiment, so there is a variable to compare the other squares to.

Ask the children if there is anything else they can do to make this a fair race or experiment; for example, use exactly 5 ml of water on each square, to make sure that one square doesn't "win" because it had less water to disappear.

3. Conduct the race, continuing until all squares have evaporated.

4. After the race, complete the observation by listing the methods which worked most rapidly in getting the squares to disappear.

Ask if anyone knows the word for the process in which water molecules seem to disappear: *evaporation.* Have a search for the word *vapor* and explain that it means matter in gas form.

5. Have the children complete the conclusion. Acceptable answers: 1, sun, wind, evaporation; 2. sun, wind; 3. clouds. Note that section 3 establishes the idea that weather depends upon an evaporation system in which solar energy and water interact. It is part of the water cycle.

Puddle Jumpers

1 2 3 Procedure

1. This requires students to create two 5 ml puddles. One puddle is spread out on a surface, while the other one remains within the 30 ml cup with a smaller surface area.

I have found it helpful to pour the first 5 ml onto a small tray or plastic plate. If the students try to spread it out with their fingers they will be removing water inadvertently and changing the variables of the experiment.

2. Explain that while this is still a race, it is a slow motion one, and will require more time to find a winner.

3. The winner of the race is the first puddle to evaporate. (Of course, *you* know that this will be the one with the greater surface area.)

During the conclusion discussion, try to get the children to infer that in the spread-out puddle, more water molecules can jump out at the same time because there are more of them at the surface. A quick sketch on the board should help.

4. Ask if anyone knows the name of the biggest "puddle" on Earth. (The Pacific Ocean.) Show the children the globe, and ask them to visualize warmed surface water molecules jumping out of the oceans into the air. They will be visualizing the system that drives Earth's weather.

Acceptable cloze answers: 1. shallow; 2. shallow, evaporate (disappear); 3. Pacific Ocean.

earth

Can Molecules Jump?

▲ **PROBLEM:** What can make water molecules jump into the air?

■ **HYPOTHESIS:** _____

● **METHOD:**

Paint 3 equal sized spots of water.

Leave one alone.

Heat one.

Fan one.

👁 **OBSERVATION:**

(List in the order of evaporation.)

1. _____

2. _____

3. _____

★ **CONCLUSION:**

1. The heat was like heat from the _____, and the fanning

   was like movement energy from the _____.

   This jumping process is called _____.

2. Energy from the _____ and _____ can make water molecules jump into the air.

3. When many water molecules jump into the air, _____ form!

e a r t h

Puddle Jumpers! (followup)

▲ **PROBLEM:** Which puddle will evaporate first—the shallow or the deep one?

■ **PREDICTION:** _____

● **METHOD:**

1. Pour 5 ml of water into 2 measuring cups.
   —Empty one onto the plate to form a shallow puddle.
   —Keep the other cup the way it is, so you have a deep 5 ml puddle. WAIT . . .

👁 **OBSERVATION:** (Try to give the time it took.)

1. _____

_____

_____

_____

_____

_____

_____

★ **CONCLUSION:**

1. The _____ puddle evaporated first.

2. More water molecules in the _____ puddle touched the air so it was easier for them to _____ into it.

3. Earth's largest puddle is the

_____.

The Love Life of Water Molecules
More Love Among the Molecules (followup)
The Water Cycle (followup)

All recommended for Grades K–4

 Lesson Overview

Explorations of water droplets will lead children to discover why raindrops form and these other . . .

 Science Principles

1. Water is both cohesive and adhesive.
2. The molecular property of cohesion is due to the bipolar nature of the water molecule. The positive end of one molecule attracts the negative end of another molecule.
3. Cohesion causes water to form a convex skin-like covering called surface tension.
4. Adhesion causes water to be attracted to other substances. This is also due to electrostatic forces.
5. Water changes from one phase to another in a cycle.

 Materials Needed

For each group
1. Two or more droppers.
2. A small, clear container of water.
3. A 5 × 5 cm square of waxed paper.

For each child
4. A paper towel.
5. Data sheet and followup sheets.

 Getting Started

1. Review the children's understanding that water molecules can jump apart from each other when they absorb energy from the sun.
2. Ask if anyone knows what happens to water molecules when they evaporate into the air. The children will undoubtedly say they gather in clouds. You can then get a laugh by asking if they hang out together because they are good friends.

   Inform the children that today they are going to find out if that joke is true. Do water molecules love each other—or in scientific terms, are they attracted to each other?
3. Before the children record their hypotheses, have them recall any real life experiences they have had with drops of water. To get them started, ask if any have noticed how water behaves on windows.

 Procedure

1. Have the children place two small drops of water on the wax paper near each other. Then have them tap the paper or lift it carefully to bring the drops nearer to each other.

   Tell the children to watch carefully when the drops are almost touching. (When the drops are close enough, they will attract each other to form a larger drop.) Expect excitement when this happens. Allow many repetitions before the children record their observation.

2. The children now investigate the shape of a drop of water by placing a drop on the waxed paper and bending down to check its profile. They should sketch the side view in observation 2.

3. During the conclusion discussion, remind the children of the way opposite poles on magnets attract each other, and ask them to visualize molecules acting as miniature magnets attracting each other. (It really is an electrical attraction, so if your students are familiar with the way a rubbed glass rod or pencil attracts small pieces of paper, you may prefer to make this comparison.)

   This is called *cohesion*. Elicit the fact that *cohesion* means the molecules are *co*operating with each other.

4. Cohesion causes water to form rounded drops because all the molecules are attracting each other and pulling into a ball. Ask what shape water drops would take in space. (Spherical.)

5. To check for understanding, ask the children to predict what a side view of the surface of the water in the container will look like. Then have them look at the container from the side. Point out that this effect is called *surface tension*.

6. Pose the question of what would happen if many water molecules were to evaporate into the air, jump high into the atmosphere, lose heat energy and slow down because they have less energy. What would happen if one airborne molecule came near another up there? (A small droplet would form. This would attract other droplets to form drops that would finally be pulled down by the force of gravity.)

Point out that the opposite of evaporation is described by the word *condensation*, which means "to gather together." Someone is bound to notice the *co* at the word's beginning.

Acceptable cloze answers:
1. attract; 2. drops, tension;
3. condensation.

7. It never hurts to finish up with a two act "molecular" drama. I call several "molecules" up to demonstrate liquid water (the children hold hands loosely), evaporation (the children jump up and down energetically, dropping hands and moving apart from each other), and condensation (the children slow down, while those closer to each other join hands and clump back together again).

More Love

 Procedure

1. The followup problem challenges the children to investigate whether water molecules are fickle and can be attracted to other kinds of molecules.

   Before the children write the hypothesis, ask them to think of their experiences with water and towels, for instance.

2. After the children place water drops on the paper toweling, ask for descriptions. Are the water drops rounded or flat? Are the water molecules attracted more to themselves or to the towel?

3. During the conclusion discussion, help children realize that water molecules can stick to other molecules, just as adhesive tape sticks to the board.

   Challenge someone to change two letters in *cohesive* to describe how water behaved in this experiment.

Towels are often called absorbent. Can anyone say what the word *absorbent* means?

4. Relate the property of water adhesion to condensation by pointing out that there are many particles of dust in the atmosphere. Lonesome jumping water molecules can be attracted to dust particles (adhesion), and then other water molecules will be attracted (cohesion) to make the droplet grow.

Acceptable cloze answers:
1. are attracted (stick); 2. cohesion; 3. atmosphere.

5. Be sure the children understand that adhesive and cohesive forces are always present with water—but certain circumstances make one force more dominant.

Point out that chemists can create detergents which lessen water's cohesive property. (You could mention "spotless" dish detergent commercials.)

Ask the children which kind of raincoat they would want to wear—one that allows water to be more cohesive or more adhesive? (Cohesive, so water is not absorbed.) Should bath towels be rough or smooth, and why?

Water Cycle

 Procedure

1. Assign this followup as homework for older children. Note that you will be dealing with the water cycle again in The Pollution Connection: Percolation (page 120) and in Landforms (page 87). Acceptable answers:
1. evaporate, oceans (etc.); 2. condense, droplets (clouds); 3. precipitation; 4. puddles, evaporates.

 Strategic Tips

1. I would save More Love Among the Molecules for a second short session.

2. A consumer science investigation into the absorbency of paper towels might be fun.

Name _____

The Love Life of Molecules!

e a r t h

▲ **PROBLEM:** Is there an attraction between molecules that are the same?

■ **HYPOTHESIS:** _____

● **METHOD:**

1. Place 2 drops of water near each other on waxed paper. Jiggle the paper to get them even closer. Watch.

2. Place a new drop of water on waxed paper. Draw a side view of it.

👁 **OBSERVATION:**

1. The water drops _____

_____

_____

_____

_____

2.

_____ waxed
paper

★ **CONCLUSION:**

1. The molecules _____ each other.

2. *C*ohesion happens when molecules cling together to form

_____. The drops have

surface _____.

3. Raindrops form because of

_____.

Name _____

More Love Among the Molecules! (followup)

e a r t h

▲ **PROBLEM:** Are water molecules also attracted to other kinds of molecules?

■ **HYPOTHESIS:** _____

● **METHOD:**

1. Place 2 drops of water on a towel.

2. Place 2 drops of water on your clothes.

👁 **OBSERVATION:**

1. _____

   _____

2. _____

   _____

★ **CONCLUSION:**

1. Water molecules _____ to other kinds of molecules.

2. Water can stick like an adhesive band-aid. This is called _____.

3. When water molecules are attracted to dust in the _____, raindrops can form.

Name _____

The Water Cycle

precipitation
evaporate   puddles clouds rivers
condense   oceans

1. Solar energy makes the water molecules _____

   from bodies of water like _____.

2. The water molecules travel up into the air, lose heat energy and

   gather together (_____) in _____.

3. The droplets in clouds grow heavier as they gather together.
   They fall down as _____ (rain, snow, sleet or hail).

4. The precipitation gathers in _____, is warmed by

   the sun, and _____ again.

Water and the Earth's Crust

Water and the Earth's Crust is *recommended for Grades 2–4, but may be adapted for K–2*

Lesson Overview

In this two-session lesson, measuring the volume and mass of water and ice leads to these "solid" . . .

Science Principles

1. The amount of matter (molecules) packed into a given volume (amount of space) determines the density of the material.

2. Water is a unique substance because it expands when frozen. Since the volume of water increases when it becomes a solid (ice or snow), its density then decreases.

3. When water goes into its solid state, molecular bonds become stronger but spaces between the molecules increase.

4. More than 4 billion years of weathering of the Earth's crust has broken many larger rocks into smaller particles. Water's expansion during freezing has contributed to this by the process of frost-wedging.

5. Solid water's decreased density enables ice to float, which in turn allows water life to survive harsh winter conditions.

Materials Needed

1. Access to a freezer.
2. A permanent marker.

3. An open container of water (such as a plastic food container).

For each group

4. A 30 ml measuring cup.

5. A small container of water (enough to fill the measuring cup).

6. A balance scale.

7. Gram cubes or standard paper clips as weights for the scale, up to 30 grams. (If you have to use paper clips, you will find that most brands weigh ½ gram each. Use brands of that mass.)

For each child

8. For the followup, a measuring cup of any size you choose.

9. Data sheet.

Getting Started

Note: The Earth's Crust procedure needs to be broken into two separate sessions of 30–40 minutes each. The best place to break is after step 4, which allows time for the water samples to freeze.

1. Review the children's knowledge that when water condenses, its molecules move closer together again. Ask for a prediction of what water molecules would do if they lost even more heat energy, slowed down, and froze. Would the molecules move even closer together?

2. While the children are hypothesizing, use a permanent marker to place a different symbol on each group's cup, so that you can return the same cup to the group for the next session.

Procedure

1. Instruct children to carefully pour 30 ml of water into their measuring cups.

2. Each group should mass their water and cup. Because the cup must be weighed, a counter-weight empty cup should be placed on the balance pan with the gram cubes (or paper clips).

3. Ask each group to share its massing information, and draw a chart on the board to enter all volumes and weights.

4. Place the cups of water in the freezer.

5. Present the cups of ice to the class.

   Have the children record the volume (they will have to write "30 plus," or state that the volume exceeds the top of the cup), and then record the mass following the method described in step 2.

   Survey the groups to record the frozen masses and volumes on the blackboard chart.

6. Ask which had to have been increased when the water froze—the number of molecules of water or the amount of empty space.

   If the children are still confused, ask which has weight—molecules or empty space. (If the water didn't gain weight when it froze and expanded, then the only thing it could gain would be empty space between the molecules.)

7. Pose the question: *What would have happened if you had frozen the water in a covered, glass container?* (It would have broken.) This may remind children of what happens to soda bottles if they are left in the freezer. Do they now know why that happened?

8. Relate the following:
   When the Earth was first formed, it was a hot ball of gases that gradually cooled off. The outer molecules pulled themselves together (condensed) and eventually became part of the solid crust. The crust was made of huge slabs of rock. But today the Earth is covered with small rocks and tiny particles of rock. How did the huge slabs break into smaller and smaller pieces?

   Draw a rock with a small crack in it, and ask the children to imagine rain getting into the crack and then freezing. What would happen to the crack? To the rock? (It would gradually widen, if the rain, freezing and thawing processes happened many times. Eventually, the large rock would become two smaller rocks. Over years, many smaller rocks would be created. This process is called *frost-wedging*.)

9. Hold up the ice from one of the frozen cups and ask if it would sink or float if placed in water. Because of its solid appearance, most children will still expect it to sink. After the predictions, place the ice in a container of water to show it does float.

   Ask: *What effect on life in ponds and oceans would floating ice have?* Draw a quick sketch of a pond, and ask the children to imagine what would happen to the animals and plants underneath if a layer of ice sank. (Clunk!)

10. Acceptable cloze answers might be: 1. room or space; weight or mass; same; no; 2. volume; break or split; smaller; frost wedging; 3. molecules; float; water; 4. they would be crushed by sinking ice (or: all of the water might freeze around them).

Water Works

▲ **PROBLEM:** How does the strange behavior of water affect the earth's crust?

2. Place in the freezer until the water becomes solid. Measure and mass the cup with water.

2. Water's volume is _____ Mass of cup and water is

_____

★ **CONCLUSION:**

1. The frozen water takes up more _____ in the cup. Water increases its volume but not its _____ when it freezes. The number of molecules is the _____, but there is more empty space between them. Empty space has

_____ weight.

2. Because water takes up more room when frozen (expands its

_____,) water can _____ rocks when it gets into cracks and freezes. The frozen water is actually able to push the rocks apart a little every time the freezing process occurs. This makes the cracks gradually get bigger, so the rock finally breaks apart into two or more smaller rocks.

This can make big rocks into _____ rocks over many years. This process is called _____.

3. Because there is more empty space between the _____ when water becomes solid, ice can _____ on top of liquid water. Ice is less dense than liquid _____.

4. This is good for underwater life such as fish and plants because

_____

H₂O—The Chemical We Call Water

Recommended for Grades 2–4

Lesson Overview

A simple chemistry experience using kitchen chemicals will lead students to discover these . . .

Science Principles

1. Chemicals can be liquids, solids, or gases.
2. Matter has chemical properties as well as physical properties. (Is the material an acid or a base?)
3. An indicator tells us about a chemical's pH by reacting and changing color. The indicator will not react with a neutral substance.
4. Pure water is chemically neutral.
5. A system occurs when two or more materials interact and are changed by that interaction.

Materials Needed

1. A piece of scrap paper.
2. Pink, green, and purple chalk.

For each group

3. A small clear container with 30 ml of red cabbage juice.
4. A medicine dropper.
5. A styrofoam half-dozen egg carton (or five test tubes) with the following in different sections:
   · 10 ml lemon juice;
   · 5 cc automatic dishwashing detergent (be sure it does not contain lemon scent or juice);
   · 10 ml vinegar;
   · 10 cc baking soda;
   · 10 ml tap water.

For each child

6. Data sheet.

Getting Started

1. Before class, create red cabbage juice by combining equal amounts of thinly sliced red cabbage and water. Heat to almost a boil and cool. Save the purple juice and discard the sliced cabbage. Store the juice in a tightly closed container (such as a rinsed soda bottle) in the refrigerator until needed.
2. The groups should receive the listed materials prior to the discussion. You do not need to label the sections of the egg cartons, but place the items in the same corresponding sections of each carton to make them easier to identify.
3. Quickly review the fact that water is a unique substance because it can be found in liquid, solid, or gaseous states at temperatures on Earth.

   Establish that when water changes phase, its molecules have not changed. Therefore this is only a physical change.

   Demonstrate a physical change by ripping or crumpling paper. The paper is still paper—but if you were to burn it, it would become ashes and no longer be paper. It would have gone through a chemical change.
4. Discuss the fact that matter has chemical properties as well as physical properties.

Ask if anyone has ever heard of the word *acid*. Ask for a description of what an acid can do. Explain that acids can be weak or strong.

1 2 3 Procedure

1. Explain that the opposite of an acid, chemically, is a base. Question the children to reinforce the idea that acids can be sour in taste, while bases can feel slippery. Then encourage the students to work cooperatively to complete the top section of the data sheet.

   Acceptable answers: 1. liquids, solids, gases; 2. acid, base, neutral; 3. 7; 4. orange (grapefruit) juice.

2. Some chemist should realize that feeling a strong base or tasting a chemical to see if it is sour (acidic) could be quite risky to one's health.

   Explain that scientists use special chemical indicators that tell (or indicate) what kind of chemical properties substances have. An indicator does so by changing color.

3. Draw a pH scale on the board, using pink chalk for the acid side and green chalk for the basic side. Use purple chalk to write the word *neutral* in the center.

   Ask if anyone can tell, by looking at the drawing of the scale, what color the purple indicator will turn if it is mixed with an acid (pink family) or a base (green family). What color will the indicator turn if the chemical is neither acid or base? (It will remain purple because it will not react in a chemical system.)

4. Name the five materials to be analyzed, and then elicit descriptions of their visible physical properties. Be sure that everyone knows which substance is which.

   Demonstrate how a chemist "wafts" an aroma safely, by placing your nose a few inches away from the chemical and waving the air over the chemical toward your nose.

   Emphasize that hands are always to be kept away from the face during a chemistry, cooking, cleaning, or art experience.

5. Tell the children they will be taking turns to place a dropper full of cabbage juice into each chemical in the egg carton. First, however, elicit predictions of any of the chemical systems (color responses) which will occur.

   For example, the children should be able to predict that lemon juice is an acid because of its similarity to (sourish) orange juice.

6. Have the children follow the procedure. They should note each system (color response) in the observation secton of the data sheet.

   When the baking soda is tested, a blue-green color will appear. Remind the children that this color should be classified as being a member of the green family.

7. For the conclusion discussion, the children should realize that any chemical which turned the cabbage juice into a shade of pink was an acid, while a shade of green signified a base. The water should have merely diluted the indicator without changing its color. Thus water is a neutral substance which can be used to dilute and weaken acids and bases.

H₂O, the Unique Chemical!

e a r t h

1. Water and other chemical substances on our Earth are found as _____, _____ and _____.

2. These substances have chemical properties as well as physical properties. Substances can have the chemical properties of being either _____, _____ or _____.

Acids	Neutral	Bases
0	7	14

3. Acids and bases are like opposites, chemically. A neutral chemical would be in the middle at #7 on the pH scale.

4. The closer a chemical is to being neutral, the weaker it is. For breakfast, you might have had a weak, slightly sour tasting acidic drink of _____.

▲ **PROBLEM:** What kind of chemical property does water have?

■ **HYPOTHESIS:** _____

● **METHOD:**

1. Add indicator to lemon juice.
2. Add indicator to vinegar.
3. Add indicator to soap powder.
4. Add indicator to baking soda.
5. Add indicator to water.

● **OBSERVATION:**

1. The system looks _____.
2. The system looks _____.
3. The system looks _____.
4. The system looks _____.
5. The system looks _____.

★ **CONCLUSION:**

1. Water is not an _____ or _____. It is _____.

The Pollution Connection: Acid Rain
Particles of Pollution (followup)

The Pollution Connection: Acid Rain is *recommended for Grades 2–4*

Particles of Science is *recommended for Grades 1–4*

Lesson Overview

In one or two classroom sessions, students explore how air, water, and pollution interact. As they create "acid rain," test the real thing, and follow up with a homework pollution "catching" activity, they discover these . . .

Science Principles

1. A chemical system occurs when two or more substances interact and are changed.
2. Life on Earth is affected by the environment.

Materials Needed

For each group of two
1. For each of the two activities, 10 ml bromothymol blue or red cabbage juice indicator. (BTB, which is preferable, can be obtained from your junior or senior high school labs or ordered inexpensively through many science supply catalogues. If you use cabbage juice, follow the instructions in the previous lesson.)
2. One clear plastic cup containing 10 ml of tap water.
3. One clear plastic cup containing 10 ml of rain water. (Collect this in advance in a large container and/or ask children to bring in "contributions" in small sealable containers.)

For each child
4. A straw.
5. For the followup, enough Vaseline to coat a 10 × 10 cm piece of paper with a thin layer.
6. Data sheet and followup sheet.

Getting Started

1. Open a discussion about air pollution and its causes. Ask the children to describe how they know when air is polluted.

    Point out that sometimes pollution is not always observable with the senses of sight or smell, but it is there, and can cause just as much damage as perceptible air pollution.
2. Explain that the children will be creating acid rain by using their breath to simulate carbon monoxide and other emissions from factories and automobiles.

Procedure

1. Explain that the two "polluters" in each group will blow through their straws into 10 ml of tap water for two minutes.
2. To test for the presence of pollution, the children will add 10 ml of bromothymol blue or cabbage juice indicator to the "polluted" water. The indicator should change color in reaction to the carbonic acid which has formed.

If you are using BTB, its blue color will turn greenish yellow in reaction to the carbonic acid. With red cabbage juice the effect will be less exciting—just a slightly pinker shade of purple.

3. The children should understand that this activity serves as a model for rain falling through polluted air and pollutants dissolving in the rain. When carbon monoxide or carbon dioxide dissolves in water, an acid called carbonic acid is formed.

4. Have the children perform the activity and complete the first section of their data sheets.

   You may wish to end the first session here, especially if you have not yet collected the rain water.

5. Distribute the rain water to the groups. Have them use the indicator of your choice to test for the presence of carbonic acid, following the method described in step 2.

6. Depending upon the area in which you teach, you may or may not have highly acidic rain. Keep in mind that all rain is slightly acidic, since it falls through air that always contains carbon dioxide, so do not be alarmed if the indicator reacts to show the presence of acid.

Particles of Pollution

 Procedure

1. As homework, ask the students to cut out the square of white paper from their followup sheet and coat it thinly with Vaseline. Using adhesive tape rolled so that it sticks on both sides, they should place the paper on an outside window at home, Vaseline side outward.

2. Choose a period when no rain is forecast and have the students leave the papers in place for several days in order to collect particulate pollution.

   Particulate pollution refers to pollutants in a form too large to be dissolved. These particles make up the grime you wash off your face after a day downtown.

3. The children then bring their papers to class and compare them for quantities of grime. Follow this grime comparison with a discussion in which the children hypothesize about the locales in which the air was tested.

   Can the children tell which paper was near a busily trafficked street? What does this tell them about the desirability of jogging on main thoroughfares?

4. Post the papers on a bulletin board, arranging them by geographical location.

 Strategic Tips

1. This topic lends itself to several useful followup activities. You could have students explore how air and water pollution affect life. Appoint Pollution Watch Reporters who clip and report on news items dealing with the causes and effects of acid rain and particulate pollution upon both plants and animals.

   Discuss protective behavior to follow when exercising outdoors during days when pollution levels are high. (Avoid strenuous exercise, keep away from pollution sources such as busy streets, etc.)

The Pollution Connection

e a r t h

▲ **PROBLEM:** What is acid rain and what causes it?

■ **HYPOTHESIS:** _____

● **METHOD:**   ☞ **OBSERVATION:**

1. Blow gently through a straw to put your extra carbon dioxide (pollution) into the water. Does it look polluted?

   1. _____

   _____

2. Test your water with the indicator. Does it change color?

   2. _____

   _____

★ **CONCLUSION:**

1. Acid ran happens when _____

Real Life Science! Is your rain water acidic?

▲ **PREDICTION:** _____

● **METHOD:**   ☞ **OBSERVATION:**

Test the rain water (10 ml) with your indicator.

_____

★ **CONCLUSION:** _____

_____

_____

Particles of Pollution

(followup)

How much particulate air pollution is in your air?
To find out follow these directions:

1. Cut out your 10 cm. × 10 cm. white square of paper.

2. Spread a thin layer of Vaseline on it.

3. Tape it, Vaseline side out, on an outside window of your house.

4. Leave it for _____ days.

5. Bring it back to school after covering it with clear wrap.

6. Compare it to your classmates'.
   Can you tell who lives in the most congested area?

   How? _____

   _____

   _____

7. Why shouldn't you exercise outdoors near busy roads? Two reasons are:

   _____

   _____

   _____

   _____

The Pollution Connection: Percolation
A Water Usage Survey (followup)

The Pollution Connection: Percolation is *recommended for Grades K–4*

Lesson Overview

Your geologists will build an underground "layer cake" of soil, sand, and pebbles to explore what happens to water that doesn't evaporate, and the pollution that threatens it. In the process they will discover these . . .

Science Principles

1. An object's properties can be affected by the size and shape of the particles of which it is composed.
2. Liquids are fluid, and change shape to fit the space in which they are contained.
3. A system occurs when two or more objects interact causing a change in the objects.
4. Life affects and is affected by the environment.

Materials Needed

For each group
1. Three small clear plastic cups about the size of a shot glass, or three test tubes.
2. Enough potting soil, sand, and small pebbles or gravel in equal parts to fill one cup or tube halfway up. (If necessary, you can obtain sand and gravel from a garden store or pet store.)
3. Enough water in the second cup to pour into the first so that it soaks in without saturating the soil, etc.
4. Half as much food coloring in the third cup as you have water in the second cup. (Choose any dark shade of coloring. Dilute it, but be sure to keep it intense.)

For each child
5. Data sheet.

Getting Started

1. Before class, as you prepare the materials, test for the amounts of soil ingredients and water needed.
2. Ask if anyone knows where their drinking water comes from. Depending upon where you live, answers might range from rivers or lakes to reservoirs or wells (or even the kitchen tap!).
3. Ask if anyone knows how old the water is that they drink. The children will be amazed to know that it is composed of water molecules which are almost as old as the Earth itself.

    Ask if anyone can explain how the same water can be used over and over again. If no one brings up the concept of *water cycle*, review it.
4. Explain that drinking water in some parts of the world comes from natural storage areas underground.

    To introduce the word *aquifer*, ask if anyone knows what the color *aqua*marine means or what an *aqua*rium holds. Perhaps someone knows the Spanish word for water—*agua*. Then ask if anyone knows now what an aquifer is.

Elicit hypotheses as to how the water got into the ground. Then inform your geologists that they are going to discover how drinking water gets into the ground and why so many communities have endangered water supplies, even if these don't come from underground.

 Procedure

1. Give time for the children to look at the supplies set upon their work surfaces. Explain that they will be placing the pebbles, sand, and soil into the empty cup so that the pebbles are at the bottom, the sand in the middle, and the soil on top. They will thus have built a layer cake of materials found in the ground.

2. Then give time for the children to brainstorm a hypothesis to the question: *Where does rain water go if it does not all evaporate?*

   Accept hypotheses such as: Into lakes, into reservoirs for drinking water, off the land into the ocean.

3. Provoke discussion about runoff pollution by offering scenarios of oil washing off streets during rainstorms, into drains, and then into bodies of water.

4. Invite the children to proceed with the first activity—building the "underground layer cake." Ask for observations of how the pebbles fit together, in contrast to the sand and soil.

   Elicit that there is more room between the pebbles because they are larger and more irregularly shaped.

5. Have the children model a rainstorm by pouring the clean water onto the "layer cake."

   Observations should make mention of the fact that the water *percolates* or trickles through the soil into the spaces between the pebbles.

   Some children may be aware of how to brew coffee, but if no one mentions it, bring up the idea that coffee is sometimes made in *percolators*—so called because boiling water trickles through the ground coffee.

6. The conclusion discussion should answer the question of underground water storage by mentioning the spaces between the pebbles filled with percolated water.

7. Remind the children of the runoff polluted water discussion (step 2 above) and ask if anyone now has a hypothesis about what is endangering wells and aquifers.

8. Tell the children that the food coloring represents acid rain, excess fertilizer, dumped chemicals, and gasoline spills.

   Have them pour this "pollution" onto the soil in the first cup. Allow time for the children to watch the pollution as it percolates through the particles of soil and ends up in the aquifer.

9. If some colored water remains on top of the soil, you have a perfect model of runoff pollution. This could be poured into a clean cup of water, which would represent a pond.

10. The conclusion discussion should include the idea that all drinking water sources are endangered by pollution.

The Pollution Connection: Percolation!

earth

Experiment One:

▲ **PROBLEM** Where can rain water go when it doesn't evaporate?

■ **HYPOTHESIS:** _____

● **METHOD:**   👁 **OBSERVATION:**

1. Build the layers under the ground. Are there any spaces?

     1. _____

2. Make it rain!

    What happens to the water?

     2. _____

★ **CONCLUSION:** Some rain water can _____

_____

This water can be used for drinking.

Experiment Two:

▲ **PROBLEM:** How is groundwater endangered?

■ **HYPOTHESIS:** _____

● **METHOD:**   👁 **OBSERVATION:**

1. Spill chemicals onto the top soil.

     1. _____

★ **CONCLUSION:** Groundwater in wells, aquifers, lakes, ponds, and streams can get polluted when _____

_____

Dirt Detectives
A Soil Investigation (followup)

Both recommended for Grades K–4

 Lesson Overview

Comparing and contrasting three types of soil will lead to the discovery of these . . .

 Science Principles

1. Soils may have different properties which make them suitable for different purposes.
2. The properties of soil are often dependent upon the size of its particles.
3. The Earth's crust has changed as interaction with water has resulted in both weathering and erosion of rocks and soil.

 Materials Needed

1. A permanent marker.
2. Enough gravel, sand, small rocks, and potting soil to create soil mixtures for the groups (see Getting Started step 1 below). If necessary, you could obtain sand and gravel from garden stores, pet stores, or toy stores.
3. A large baking pan filled with sand.
4. Several newspapers to catch mess.
5. Several medicine droppers.
6. A large pitcher or watering can.
7. A globe.
8. Any rootbound house plant other than a cactus.

For each group
9. Three-section paper plate.

10. A clear empty tennis ball can, lid included, label removed, filled halfway with water.
11. A small chunk of dried clay.

For each child
12. Data sheet and followup sheet.

 Getting Started

1. Before class, use your marker to label each section of each paper plate "Sample 1," "Sample 2," and "Sample 3," near the depressions. Then place the following soil mixtures in each section:
   · Sample 1: mostly gravel, with a few grains of sand and a few small rocks.
   · Sample 2: mostly sand, with a few small rocks.
   · Sample 3: mostly potting soil, with a few small rocks scattered in.
2. Show the children the globe and ask for a volunteer to point out a seacoast. Elicit that the seacoast is where water and land meet. Ask for other examples of places where water and land meet—for instance, a river bank, or any land during a rainstorm. Then tell the children that today they are going to explore what happens when water and land meet.
3. Show the children the sand in the baking pan. Have a quick discussion about where this type of soil might be found. Explain that this experiment could be done with other types of soil, but this is the least messy for the classroom.
4. Invite some "rainmakers" up to create a rainy day on the sand by

using the medicine droppers and water. Have them squeeze the droppers gently at first, and then release larger drops. Discuss the changes made by the water, eliciting that some sand was moved by the rain.

5. Have the children predict what would happen if a large amount of water were poured across the sand. Tilt pan at a slight downward angle, and pour water from the pitcher or watering can so it resembles a stream. Discuss the fact that water carries sand along as it scoops out a "riverbed." Explain that this process is called *erosion*.

 Procedure

1. If anyone has visited a beach, ask for a description of the waves' actions. Give each group a tennis ball can half filled with water. You could then refer to the globe to select ocean or sea names for the bodies of water.

2. Place a few grains of sand from the baking pan into each "ocean." Hold up a chunk of the clay and explain that each ocean will also receive a special "rock." Place the rocks in and cap the cans securely.

3. Announce that the rocks need some "wave action." At your signal, each child in the group will have a turn shaking the can. (No more than 10 seconds each is necessary.)

4. Have the children complete the Dirt Detectives data sheet. Ask for descriptions of the water (muddy, like chocolate milk) and ask what happened to the rock. Explain that the wave's energy "weathered" the rock. Ask if anyone knows where sand comes from now.

    After this activity, inform the children that the rock was really a special type of soil called clay, and that many, many years are required for waves to create sand from rocks. They used the clay as a model—a simpler and more convenient substitute for the real thing—as scientists frequently do.

Soil Investigation

 Procedure

1. Collect the "oceans" and distribute the plates containing the three types of soil.

    Remind the children that they understand that small particles of soil can be weathered from larger ones. Now they will be looking at and feeling three different types of soil to see what kind of particles these contain and to determine which will be best for repotting their plant. (Hold up the rootbound classroom plant.)

2. Model the feeling of textures by first gently running your finger across the entire plate section and then gently rubbing a pinch of each sample between thumb and index finger. The latter leaves extremely small particles of silt on the fingers, providing helpful information for the "size" sentences.

3. After the children share their choice for the plant's new soil, pull your plant out of the pot. Not only can the children see what kind of soil should be used (Sample 3) but they will also be able to answer this question: *What part of a plant prevents erosion?*

Dirt Detectives

earth

▲ **PROBLEM:** How do big rocks become small pieces of soil?

★★ **What to do:**
1. Place the large rock into the "ocean."
2. Make waves.

★★ **What happened:**

1. The clear water got _____.

2. The big rock _____.

★★★ **Now I know** that some big rocks become small when water

_____.

This is called _____.

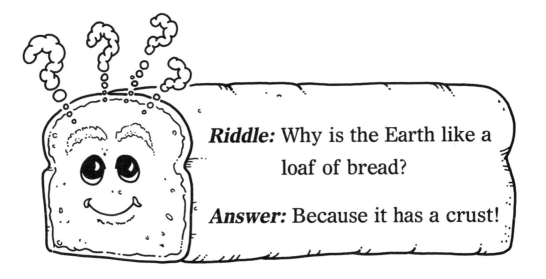

Riddle: Why is the Earth like a loaf of bread?

Answer: Because it has a crust!

A Soil Investigation

The Earth's crust is made of different kinds of soils.

▲ **PROBLEM:** Which soil is best for our plant?

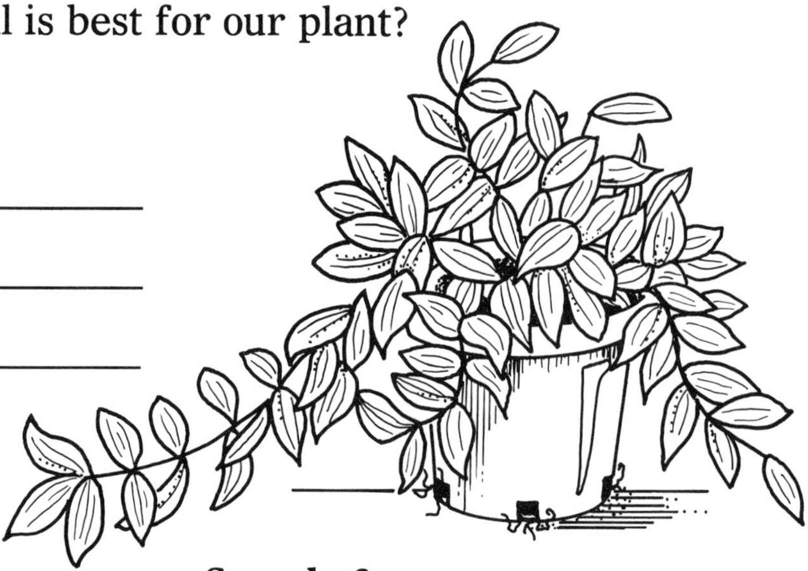

Sample 1

▲ The pieces are _____

● They feel _____

◆ They look mostly _____

Sample 2

▲ The pieces are _____

● They feel _____

◆ They look _____

Sample 3

▲ The pieces are _____

● They feel _____

◆ They look mostly _____

★ **CONCLUSION:** Sample _____ is best for our plant.

▲	●	◆
smallest bigger biggest	smooth gritty bumpy	brown beige gray

Soil—It's a Natural!

e a r t h

Recommended for Grades 2–4

 Lesson Overview

Children will compare the water absorbing properties of two different types of soil and discover these . . .

 Science Principles

1. The ability of a soil to retain water can be affected by the size and origin of solid particles contained within the soil.
2. Soil can be changed by interacting with water and/or plants or animals.

 Materials Needed

1. Enough potting soil, sand, rocks, twigs, dead leaves, and seeds such as maple samaras or acorns to provide soil samples for class demonstration and for each group (see Getting Started step 1 for details).
2. Two containers for the demonstration soil samples (large enough for the class to easily see the soil surface).

For each group

3. A divided paper plate labeled "X" and "Y," with soil samples.
4. Four 30 ml measuring cups.
5. Two 5 ounce paper cups, each with four nail holes of equal size punched into the bottom. One cup is marked "X" and the other "Y."
6. A flask of water.

For each child

7. Data sheet.

 Getting Started

1. Before class, prepare the following soil mixtures for the demonstration containers and for the group plates:
   · Soil X: potting soil into which you have mixed the seeds, twigs, and dead leaves.
   · Soil Y: sand, rocks, and a small amount of potting soil.
2. Ask if anyone knows what a *natural resource* is and where it comes from. The root word of *natural* will provide a clue.)
3. Create a word map on the board listing natural resources elicited during the discussion. Be sure that soil is named. Elicit why soil is a natural resource. Can the children think of anything they use that doesn't depend on the Earth's soil? (For example, most plastics are made from petroleum, which comes from the ground.)

   Challenge the children to find interactions or connections between the resources listed. Draw lines, for example, from soil to plants and animals.

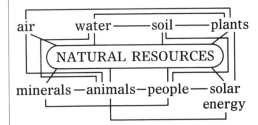

4. Stage a demonstration in which the following question is answered: *How can the atmosphere interact with the natural resource of soil?*

Call up a volunteer "wind" to blow on Soil Y and note the *erosion* (moving of soil) that takes place. If you live near a beach, desert, or dusty area, remind the children of getting sand or dust in their eyes on a windy day.

Ask: *Is there any natural resource which will prevent the erosion of the sand?* (Plants and their roots would hold the soil.)

 Procedure

1. Ask: *Do you think you can determine where the soil samples came from?* Have the children cite examples of items quickly spotted in the soils to back up their verbal hypothesis.

2. Sketch the chart at the top of the data sheet on the board. Point out that the particles seem to be listed from large to small.

   Explain that *organic evidence* refers to anything that comes from something (animal or plant) that is or was alive.

3. Model how to use the chart on the worksheet with an imaginary sample. Show how to take a pinch of soil and feel it between the fingers to determine the size of its particles.

4. Allow the children 4–5 minutes to note their observations and comparisons on their charts.

5. Ask them to use their chart to see if they still agree with their hypothesis of where the soil samples came from. You may wish to give some time to a cooperative group discussion in which evidence is cited from the chart.

6. Have a child read the problem on the work sheet. Allow time to discuss hypotheses after recalling where they thought the samples came from. Explain that this experiment will be like a race to see which soil can hold onto the *most* water.

7. Each group receives two 30 ml measuring cups, one filled with soil X and the other filled with soil Y. The children should pour these carefully into the appropriately labeled paper cups with nail holes.

8. Each paper cup with soil is then placed atop a 30 ml measuring cup, which will catch any water draining through the soils.

Hole-punched cup with sample soil and water

30 ml measuring cup to catch water draining from soil above

9. Have the children measure out 25 ml of water into the two remaining measuring cups. At your signal, have them pour the water into each soil sample. They should write immediate observations and then, after waiting 3 minutes, measure the amount of water that has drained through.

10. Before the "geologists" complete the conclusion, remind them that the winning soil will have the *least* amount of water draining into the cup at the end of three minutes.

   The soil with silt and organic particles will hold water longer. The water will be absorbed by the organic materials, and the close fit of the small particles will make it harder for water to drain through to the measuring cup.

Soil—It's a Natural!

earth

Soil Analysis Chart

Compare and contrast the 2 soil samples. Write more, less, or equal.

Material in Soil	Sample X	Sample Y
Large rock particles		
Small rock particles		
Sand (feels gritty)		
Silt (feels smoother)		
Organic evidence		

▲ **PROBLEM:** Which soil sample will hold water longer?

■ **PREDICTION:** Sample _____ will, because it has

_____ particles.
(smaller or larger)

● **METHOD:**

1. Pour 25 ml of water over samples X and Y.

2. Wait 3 minutes and measure the water that drains.

👁 **OBSERVATION:**

1. Sample X _____

   Sample Y _____

2. _____ ml drained from X.

   _____ ml drained from Y.

★ **CONCLUSION:**

1. Sample _____ held water longer.

2. The particles in the winning soil were _____ than the losing soil's particles.

✱ **EXTRA! EXTRA!** On the back make a word map showing 10 or more products that depend on soil.

A Mineral Mystery

Recommended for Grades 2–4 as written. Can be adapted for Grades K–1

 Lesson Overview

Testing the physical properties of minerals with household items, and reading a chart deductively, will lead mineralogists to these . . .

 Science Principles

1. Different kinds of materials have different physical properties.
2. Some properties of objects depend upon the materials from which they are made.

 Materials Needed

1. A dozen toothpicks.
2. 8–10 gumdrops or small blobs of plasticine clay, half of them one color and half another color.
3. A small amount of kosher (large crystal) salt.

For each group

4. A small box with cover (to contain items 5 through 8).
5. A streakplate or small white unglazed ceramic tile.
6. A small sample of each mineral you choose to use: talc; mica (muscovite or biotite); halite; sulfur; calcite; galena; quartz. (These samples can be purchased very inexpensively in bags of 10 through science supply catalogues. Streakplates can also be ordered.)

7. A penny.
8. A steel nail.

For each child

9. Data sheet.

 Getting Started

1. Before class, construct a toothpick and plasticine or gumdrop model of a crystal of salt. Use two different colors alternately to represent the sodium and chlorine atoms in the crystal. Do not finish the entire pattern—have one atom missing from an outside corner.

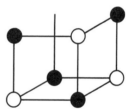

2. If you can, borrow some impressive mineral samples to display as inspirational visual aids in front of the class.
3. Place a sample of each mineral you choose to use, together with a penny, steel nail, and streakplate or tile in each group's "Mystery Box."

 Procedure

1. Remind the children that they know that the Earth's crust is basically made of rocks of different sizes. Today they will begin to solve the mystery of what those rocks—even the smallest ones—are made of.

2. Intrigue them by picking up a Mystery Box and moving it slowly so they can hear the objects inside. Inform the children that they are going to be detectives who deduce what is in their box.

   Ask if anyone can infer at least one property of an object in the box from the sound. Accept replies such as "solid" and "hard" which can be inferred from sound. If an answer refers to appearance, ask how the child was able to make that particular observation.

3. Show the children the model of the salt crystal, and ask if anyone can tell what is missing from it. Elicit that they can tell by detecting the model's pattern.

4. Sprinkle some salt crystals on each table, and ask for a description and best guess of the substance's name. Inform them that the toothpick model is really an atomic model of salt.

   Elicit a description of the properties of the salt: It is solid, and its atoms are arranged in a pattern that is reflected on the large scale we can see. Additionally, the salt is not alive.

   Allow each student to place one crystal on his or her tongue. Then inform the children that not only do they know now what a mineral is, but they have also just eaten a mineral from the Earth's crust!

5. Ask if anyone can now deduce what rocks really are made of. Some detective should know the answer is *minerals*. To reinforce this, use the following analogy: A rock is like a sentence, its minerals are like the words in the sentence, and its atoms like letters in the word.

6. Invite the detectives to open the boxes and carefully observe the contents. Ask if anyone now can deduce what is in the box.

   Ask if all the minerals are the same kind, and if not, what properties might help distinguish them from each other.

7. Inform the children that, like all good detectives, they are going to need some clues and tests to find out which mineral is which.

   Clues a geologist would use are written on the data sheet, but they must be checked out before a positive identification of the mineral suspects is made.

8. Review the data sheet categories, while you model how to use the testing equipment in the boxes. A fingernail, penny, nail, and streakplate are used to determine how hard each mineral is. Show how to move the sharp edge of one of the first three "tools" against the smooth edge of a mineral, using some pressure. Then wet your finger to remove any dust, and inspect for a scratch in the mineral's surface.

   Moh's Scale of Hardness assigns a fingernail 2½, a copper coin 3, the steel nail 5, and the edge of the streakplate 6 in scratching ability. Write these on the board for reference.

   Refer the children to the data sheet. Ask which mineral listed will test out to be the hardest (quartz), and which will be the softest (mica and talc). Ask: *Which minerals can be scratched by a penny but not by a fingernail? (Calcite and galena.) Which minerals have the same hardness—and how can they be told apart? (Calcite and galena again; by their appearance.)*

9. Refer the children to the Streak column, and show how to firmly rub the mineral against the streakplate to see if a color is left upon the tile. A clue is given for sulfur (yellow) and galena (gray).

10. The *luster* of a metal refers to its shine, and it can be described as glassy, metallic, dull, earthy, or silky. Several clues are given in that category, as well.

11. *Crystal habit* refers to the mineral's most common outer shape.

    A *planar* habit means the crystal splits along one plane—or actually peels off. (You will have mica peeling off constantly.)

    The calcite sample looks like a rhombohedron—or a squashed rectangle to the children.

    The galena and halite are vaguely recognizable cubes, while the quartz is hexagonal—especially when viewed from top or bottom.

12. Two additional clues are offered for a taste and odor test. Give the children the information that sulfur smells slightly like rotten eggs.

    Demonstrate how to taste a mineral by wetting your index finger, touching it to the mineral, and then touching your tongue. Halite, which is salt, will taste salty. (Most children are reluctant to test rocks even by this safe method, but you may wish to **emphasize that rocks are not for chewing.**)

13. Inform the children that their job is to work with their team to place each mineral next to its name on the paper. They should do this *only* after they have tested it for hardness, checked its streak, observed the luster and crystal habit, and used their senses of taste and smell.

    Only one data sheet should be used for placing the minerals, but all detectives should participate in the testing process.

14. If you are using all the minerals suggested, it is best to circulate through the room and let the children know what is correct and incorrect as they go along.

15. If some groups finish before others, those detectives can visually select a mineral and write a geological description in complete sentences on the back of their data sheet. They should then exchange sheets with a neighbor and figure out which mineral is being described.

 Strategic Tips

1. If you are working with younger children, use only a few minerals and proceed step by step with them through the testing process.

    Sketch out an abbreviated data sheet model on the board, and have them record the hardness and streak by using colored chalk.

2. For grades 2 and 3, you may wish to make an abbreviated version of the data sheet, so the children can still have practice reading a chart.

3. As a followup to the activity, you could lead the children to research the sources and uses of the minerals tested.

4. Many children will be curious to know what mineral is the hardest on Earth. Some will know it is the diamond. (Caution them not to test any jewels!)

Mineral Mystery

e a r t h

Minerals	Moh's Scale of Hardness?	Streak: Color?	Luster: Is it glassy, metallic, dull, earthy?	Crystal Habit	Taste?	Odor?
Talc	1–2		dull	none		
Mica	2		glassy	planar (flat)		
Halite	2–2½		dull	cubic	salty	
Sulfur	2½	yellow	dull	varied		rotten egg
Calcite	2–3		glassy	rhombohedron		
Galena	2-3	gray	metallic	cubic		
Quartz	7		glassy	hexagonal		

Earth—Cracking The Crust
Making Pangaea (followup)

Both recommended for Grades 1–4

 Lesson Overview

Teach plate tectonic theory with a simple demonstration in which stomping feet, water, and a model of the Earth's crust lead students to these . . .

 Science Principles

1. Energy can travel through objects.
2. A group of interacting objects is called a system.
3. When energy and objects interact, the properties of the objects may change—for instance, landforms may be created or destroyed.

 Materials Needed

1. A globe.
2. Brown, blue, red, and yellow chalk.
3. A clear tub of water (plastic shoe box size is fine).
4. Enough red food coloring to turn the tub of water a strong shade of red.
5. A styrofoam dinner plate cut into two or three puzzle pieces.
6. A dead basketball or other similar sized ball, cut into sections that remain joined only around the "equator," so that it lies flat.

For each child

7. One 8 × 11 inch sheet of blue construction paper.
8. Scissors.
9. Paste or glue.
10. Data sheet and two copies of the followup sheet.

 Getting Started

1. Before class, mix the food coloring into the tub of water. Also make sure that the globe is prominently visible.
2. Ask the children to brainstorm words beginning with the prefix *geo*. Make a list on the board, and ask for definitions—which should lead the children to realize that *geo* refers to Earth.

   Elicit that *geology* means the study of the Earth and its history, while *geography* refers to the mapping of the Earth's surface features.
3. Discuss the importance of knowing about the Earth. Elicit that people are affected by its changing environments, changes in life through evolution, climate, earthquakes, and economic value (minerals, petroleum, etc.).
4. Explain that the children have been looking at small portions of the Earth's crust, and now they are going to take a step back to look at the larger picture.

   Do they think the Earth has always looked the same? Elicit that human-made changes, weathering and erosion, and earthquakes have made changes in the Earth's crust.

5. Inform the children that they are going to perform an experiment which will explain changes that have taken place over millions of years.

6. Draw a cross-section of the Earth on the board. Use brown chalk for the crust, blue to fill in oceans, red for the mantle, yellow for the inner core, and yellow mixed with red for the outer core.

   Elicit the names *crust* and *core* for the outermost and innermost sections of the Earth by drawing an analogy between bread and apples. Explain that the mantle is molten rock and the crust floats on it.

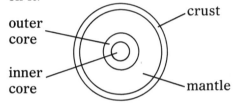

   The crust is about 21 miles (35 km) thick on land and 2–4 miles (3–7 km) thick under the oceans.

   The mantle is composed of very hot, molten rock upon which the crust floats.

   The very hot core has an outer part which is liquid and a denser, solid inner part.

7. Display the tub of red colored water, and ask if anyone can tell what section of the Earth the colored water represents. (The hot liquid mantle.)

8. Hold up the pieces of the styrofoam plate and explain that scientists liken the Earth's crust to the shell of a hardboiled egg that has dropped. The large pieces are like what we eat our dinner on—*plates*—while the cracks between the plates are called *faults*.

   Mention that scientists noticed that the continents look like a jigsaw puzzle. They also noticed that certain animals and fossils appear on different continents thousands of miles apart. How did these get from one continent to the other?

Procedure

1. Have the children circle the demonstration table where you have placed the water tub. Be sure no one actually touches the table.

2. Lay the pieces of styrofoam (fitted together) on top of the "mantle" water, and ask the children to pretend they have gone back in time millions of years. Now these "plates" fit together like a jigsaw puzzle. Do the children think the pieces will fit together like this forever?

3. Ask the children to visualize spaghetti in boiling water. Ask for a description of how the energy of the boiling water moves the spaghetti.

   Explain that the mantle is so hot that it has a tremendous amount of heat energy. This energy builds up pressure which is released in the energy of movement, rather like the energy of boiling water. Do children think that this energy within the Earth might affect the crust?

4. Instead of boiling water, stomping feet will create sound and movement energy to represent the forces of heat and pressure inside the Earth's mantle. Have the children stamp their feet and observe what happens to the Earth's crust (water) as they do so.

   Ask: *Did the energy from your feet travel? Where?* (Through the mantle and into the crust, causing it to vibrate.) *What would people who live near a fault expe-*

rience when the mantle releases pressure? (An earthquake.)

5. Have the children place their hands side by side, press them together, and then move them back and forth. Do they feel their hands "catch" on each other and then move forward in a small jump?

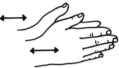

Their hands are acting as Earth's plates often do. When plates under pressure catch on each other, they will eventually "jump"—that is, cause an earthquake. The more the plates "catch," the greater the magnitude of the earthquake. However, the plates can also slip past each other without catching.

Have the children move their hands so one hand slips over the other, and ask if anyone can think of a geologic feature which would be created by the edge of one plate resting atop another. (The Himalayan Mountain range is still being created by this kind of tectonic movement.)

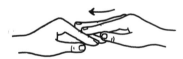

6. Allow the children to proceed to steps 3 and 4 on the data sheet, which is really a review of erosion caused by moving air and water.

7. The conclusions can be worked on in cooperative groups. (Acceptable answers: 1. has; 2. hasn't, solid (also very large). Sometime during the conclusion discussion, ask the children which Earth changing processes

probably happen faster—plate movements or erosion?

Making Pangaea

 Procedure

1. Show the children the cut-apart ball and ask them to visualize how the ball looked before it was cut.

   Hold up a copy of the continental outline world map and ask if anyone can now explain how a map of the world can be drawn.

2. Each child should receive two continental outline maps and one sheet of blue construction paper.

3. Older children can research and label one of the maps with the names of the continents and oceans of the world as a homework or independent work assignment.

   Complete this step in class with younger students.

4. The other map is to be cut apart and pasted together onto the blue paper to recreate Earth's surface millions of years ago, when the plates fitted together.

   Explain that *Pangaea* means all lands.

5. After the children display their maps of Pangaea, ask if anyone can now explain why fossils of similar animals are found on continents millions of miles apart.

 Strategic Tips

1. If your class is very large, you may need to have groups of children take turns around the water tub during the "earthquake."

2. Warn your next door neighbors so that they do not panic as the foot stomping vibrations travel into their room.

Earth—Cracking the Crust

e a r t h

▲ **PROBLEM:** Has the Earth's crust always appeared the way it does now?

■ **HYPOTHESIS:** _____

● **METHOD:**

1. Observe the pieces (plates) of the Earth's crust.

2. Stamp your feet to cause and simulate energy and movement in the mantle.

3. Blow "wind" on the crust.

4. "Rain" on the crust.

👁 **OBSERVATION:**

1. The plates fit together like a

   _____.

2. The vibrations from our feet

   _____

   _____

   _____

3. _____

4. _____

★ **CONCLUSION:**

1. The Earth _____ changed slowly because
    has or hasn't

   _____

2. The Earth's crust _____ changed more quickly because
   has or hasn't

   _____

Name _____

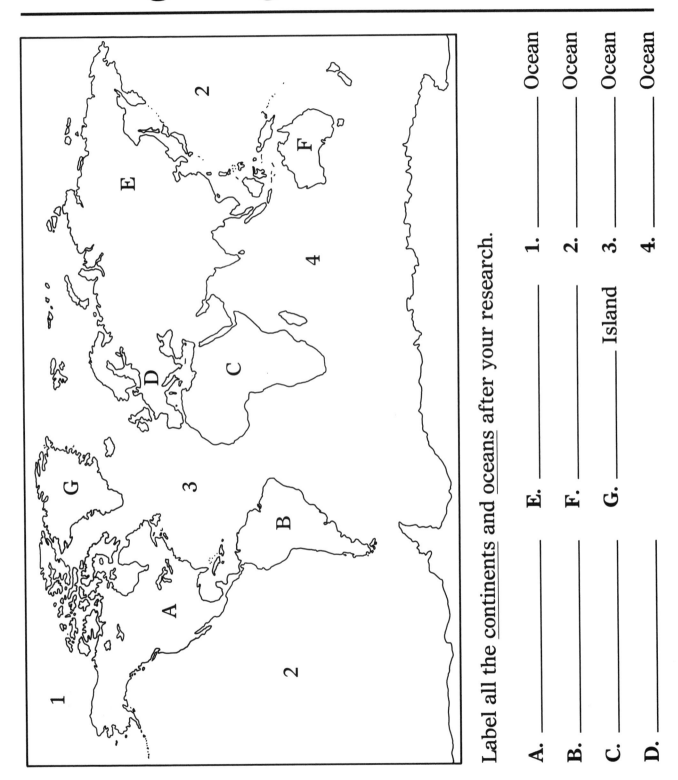

Making Pangaea

Label all the <u>continents</u> and <u>oceans</u> after your research.

A. _____

B. _____

C. _____

D. _____

E. _____

F. _____

G. _____ Island

1. _____ Ocean

2. _____ Ocean

3. _____ Ocean

4. _____ Ocean

Catch The Wave!

earth

Recommended for Grades K–4

Lesson Overview

Your oceanographers will recreate the movement and power of Earth's oceans and discover these . . .

Science Principles

1. A system occurs when two or more objects interact.
2. When energy interacts with objects in a system, the properties of the objects may be changed. (For example, wave action causes weathering and erosion on beaches.)
3. Energy exists in many forms and can travel through matter.
4. Friction occurs when two substances rub against each other.

Materials Needed

1. Samples of sharp-edged rocks and water-smoothed rocks.

For each group
2. A water container, such as a clear plastic shoebox.

For each child
3. Data sheet.

Getting Started

1. Pass around your samples of smooth and sharp rocks. Ask if anyone can tell which came from an ocean (or lake) and which came from your garden. Elicit

that the smoother ones are from water by reminding the children of the Dirt Detectives experiment (page 124) in which they shook hardened clay in a can of water.
2. Ask if anyone knows what causes the waves that weather rocks into smoothness. Allow time to share hypotheses.

   Someone is bound to come up with a hypothesis connecting the idea of wind and waves. When this happens, invite the children to test the hypothesis.

Procedure

1. Allow time for the children to observe the water in their "ocean" (container) on a windless day.
2. Have the children blow gently on the surface of the water. Tiny ripples should appear on the water's surface. Draw them on the board, and ask what kind of line you've drawn. (A wavy one.)
3. Have the children predict what will happen to the water if they blow like a hurricane. Then allow them to blow as hard as they can across the water.
4. The concluding discussion should state that wind energy is changed into the water's energy.

   The more the wind blows, the more the water is pushed along by the friction between the water and air.

   Acceptable cloze answers:
   1. system; 2. the wind blows;
   3. the bigger the waves; 4. calm.

e a r t h

Catch the Wave!

▲ **PROBLEM:** What causes waves in the ocean?

■ **HYPOTHESIS:** _____

● **METHOD:**

1. Leave the "ocean" alone.

2. Blow gently onto and across the surface.

3. Blow harder.

👁 **OBSERVATION:**

1. The water _____.

2. The water _____
   _____

3. _____

★ **CONCLUSION:** Water and wind act together like a _____

1. The ocean has waves when _____.

2. The greater the wind, _____.

3. If there is no wind, the water will be _____.

✱ **EXTRA! EXTRA!**

How can rough, wavy water change the Earth's crust? _____

_____

_____

_____

_____

Go With the Flow: Ocean Currents

e a r t h

Recommended for Grades 2–4

 Lesson Overview

Hot blue water swirling through cold water helps your oceanographers to realize why the oceans have currents and to understand these . . .

 Science Principles

1. A system occurs when two or more objects interact.
2. Energy exists in many forms and can travel through matter.
3. The density of a substance changes when it is heated or cooled.
4. Living things are affected by the environment.

 Materials Needed

1. A globe.
2. A heat source for heating water.
3. An open pot or pan in which to heat water.
4. Blue or green food coloring.
5. Source of cold water.

For each group

6. A water container. (The clear plastic shoebox is fine, again.)
7. A marble.
8. A 30 ml measuring cup or other small container for hot water.
9. A piece of clear plastic wrap.

For each child

10. Data sheet.

✓ **Getting Started**

1. Before class, stir the food coloring into a pot half full of water and start heating it.
2. Remind the children of the experiment in which a balloon placed on a bottle became inflated when heated. (See Air: It Matters to Us All, page 91.)

   Elicit the fact that the density of air decreases when its molecules are heated because they move more rapidly and spread apart. Being less dense, they rise. This causes currents of air we call wind to move in and take the place of the heated air.
2. Show the children the globe. Ask which area of the world gets the most solar energy and would have ocean temperatures that would be pleasant to swim in all year round.

   Explain that the oceans, like the air, also have currents or streams. These travel from the equator, where it is hot, toward the polar regions, where it is very cold.

   Sometimes ocean water is much warmer than might be expected because of these warm water currents. They help to warm any land near them, making it a pleasant place to live.

   Explain that today the children are going to explore what causes the currents to flow from warmer to cold regions on Earth.

Procedure

1. Half fill each group's large container with cold water.

2. Place a marble in each small container to stabilize it. Then pour in some of the hot colored water and cover with plastic wrap. Use a pencil to poke a hole through the wrap. Distribute the containers to the groups of children.

3. The children should place the hot water container on the bottom of the cold water container. They will observe warm water move into the cold by swirling up through the hole in the plastic wrap and out in a current.

4. Invite the children to slowly turn the larger container (with the container of hot colored water still in it) to simulate the Earth's spinning. This will help them understand that it is rotation which gives the currents the directions they follow.

5. During the concluding discussion, establish that the hot water was a model for equatorial waters traveling through the colder water in a current. Acceptable answers: 1. warms; 2. colder; 3. rotating (spinning); 4. system.

6. Be sure to remind the children, once again, of the hot air experiment (page 91) so they understand that the hot water behaves like air when it is heated. Water's density also decreases as it is heated, allowing it to become buoyant and float on top of the denser cold water.

7. Ask the children to predict what will eventually happen to the blue (warm) water currents as they cool off. (They sink and contribute to the circulation of the world's water.)

8. London is farther north than Buffalo, New York (or Chicago, Minneapolis, etc.), yet it is much warmer. Show the location of London, and mention that there is a warm current called the North Atlantic Current which flows nearby.

Challenge the children to explain what causes the climate to be warmer in London. (The heat from the water is transferred to the winds coming off the Atlantic.)

 Strategic Tips

1. During the first part of the lesson, check the water on the heater to make sure it does not become hot enough to burn. Turn off the heat or dilute it with cold water as necessary.

2. This lesson can lead to many possible followups. Have older children research the many warm and cold currents which travel through the world's oceans. They can sketch the paths of the currents onto their world maps.

3. Children can explore the effect of currents upon climate further by answering this question: *Besides London, what areas of the world should experience cold climates but don't, due to winds which come from warm ocean currents?*

4. Children could report on, and create a scrapbook of, animals and plants which make use of currents to travel great distances.

e a r t h

Go With the Flow

▲ **PROBLEM:** What causes ocean currents?

■ **HYPOTHESIS:** A current is a moving stream of water in the ocean caused by

_____

● **METHOD:**

1. Place the cup of hot, colored water in the bottom of the cold "ocean."

2. Gently turn the ocean.

👁 **OBSERVATION:**

1. The colored water _____

_____

_____

2. The colored water _____

_____

★ **CONCLUSION:**

1. The sun _____ ocean waters near the equator.

2. The warmer currents move into the _____ waters

    toward the North and South _____

3. The direction of the current's movements depends on the

    Earth's _____ movement.

4. When 2 or more parts of the Earth work together, that is a

    _____.

Landforms: A Geographic Expedition

Recommended for Grades K–4

 Lesson Overview

In two sessions, crunch teaching time by integrating science, social studies, creative writing, and measurement skills. This happens as students create torn paper maps with geographic features and build three-dimensional models of landforms with a working model of the water cycle, thus discovering these . . .

 Science Principles

1. The Earth's crust is composed of plates upon which geographic features have changed and will continue to change over long periods of time.
2. These landforms compose part of our environment and have influenced the history of peoples and the lives they lead.

 Materials Needed

1. A source of water. (If possible, a large container of water lightly tinted blue with food coloring.)
2. A roll of clear plastic wrap.

For each group

3. A clear plastic shoebox or similar watertight container.
4. A large enough lump of earth-colored plasticine to completely cover the bottom of the container to a depth of one inch.
5. A plastic centimeter ruler.

6. A graduate cylinder or measuring cup that holds at least 100 ml.

For each child

7. Paste or glue.
8. One 8 × 11 inch sheet of blue construction paper.
9. One half sheet of brown construction paper.
10. Scraps of white (or beige), green, and orange construction paper.
11. One or two lined index cards.
12. Review sheets.

Session One

 Getting Started

1. Explain that today the children are going to discover an island no one has ever seen before. Because they are the first to see it, they have the privilege of both naming it and developing it as a vacation hideaway. But first they have to explore and map the island and understand its geographic features.
2. Use the data review sheet to introduce your "explorers" to such terms as 1. peninsula; 2. cape; 3. bays, gulfs; 4. plain; 5. island; 6. lake; 7. mountains; 8. river; 9. slope, shelf; 10. trench; 11. mountains.

 Procedure

1. Inform the class that flights over the island have revealed a large range of geographic features, such as a peninsula, a mountain

range with a river flowing down between two mountains, lakes, a harbor or bay, a cape, a lake, a plain covered with grass, and a beautiful beach.

Write the landforms you require upon the board for the children's reference.

2. Using the brown paper, the children can first lightly sketch an outline of the island containing the features that determine its shape. Then they can cut out the island.

They next paste the island upon the larger blue (ocean) sheet.

3. The children can cut out scraps of blue paper (from the edge) to glue upon the brown paper for lakes and rivers. They can cut out and glue white or beige paper upon parts of the outer edges of the island for beaches. They can tear or cut green construction paper to simulate grassy plains. They can fold strips of orange paper accordion-style to create three-dimensional mountain ranges.

4. The children should then place on the map a key or legend which includes small squares of the colors used. They should also add a compass rose and a scale of distance.

5. When the map is complete, the children can create an advertisement extolling the virtues of their island. The ad can entice vacationers to visit an island where they can "Ski upon the snow-capped mountains . . . Anchor and swim in calm bays and harbors . . . Ride the rapids in the river . . . Sail upon blue, sparkling lakes. . . ."

The children should place this travelogue upon the index card and then glue the card close to the edge of the blue "ocean" paper.

Session Two

 Getting Started

1. Before class, line each container with clear plastic wrap or waxed paper to facilitate removal of the plasticine from the containers during cleanup.

For Procedure step 4, you will have to predetermine how much water is needed to make the construction of the model challenging.

2. This activity is best handled in small cooperative groups, because a lot of brainstorming will take place. Select groups you feel are well balanced, rather than rely merely upon seating arrangements.

3. Many children have the misconception that islands either float around on top of oceans or are anchored like boats. This activity is designed to show that islands and continents are merely higher elevations of land with lower elevations filled in by ocean. Be sure the children understand that a continent really is a very large island.

Ask the children what they think an island would look like underwater, if they could view it from the side. Discuss their theories.

Also discuss their theories of ocean floor terrain, before they proceed to the review sheet (items 9 and 10).

4. Explain that today they are going to create islands or continents and the ocean floor the way these really are, as part of the Earth's crust.

Procedure

1. The first step in creating the model is for the groups to use the plasticine to make small "silver dollar" size pancakes and place them upon the bottom of their clear plastic containers. Since these pancakes represent the plates of Earth's crust, the children should place them touching each other, like a completed jigsaw puzzle, creating "fault lines."

2. Have the children build small mounds upon the ocean floor to create high and low areas such as trenches, mountain ranges, volcanoes, etc.

3. The groups are then to build at least one large mound of plasticine atop a section of the pancake crust. This will be the island or continent. It should slope down gently at first and then sharply, to simulate the continental slope and shelf.

   Tell the groups that they are to create geographic features on the top surface of their continent. You may wish to give each group a different set of required geographic features, so they create unique land masses.

   Expect much brainstorming to occur within the groups as the children discover how to create lakes (thumbprint depressions in clay) or rivers (pencil grooves channeled into mountains).

4. Inform the children that their island or continent will have to be tall enough to project above sea level. Appoint someone in each group to come up and measure out the volume of water their ocean must contain.

5. After creating the landform masses, the children must pour the correct volume of ocean into the plastic container. If their land mass remains above sea level, they have succeeded. If not, give time to correct the situation.

   They can then pour water into lake depressions. They can also fill droppers to rain upon mountains, and watch the water run down the river beds they channeled into the plasticine.

6. The children can hold a centimeter ruler vertically to chart the depth of the ocean floor in the trenches and to measure the height of the tallest mountain on the landform.

7. They should place this information on an index card, which they then attach to an outer wall of the plastic shoe box. Beside it they should write the name of their island continent.

8. To create a working model of the water cycle, have the groups cover the top of their shoe box with plastic wrap. They should place the model, with the water in it, in the sun. Allow time for evaporation and condensation to occur. If the condensation gets heavy enough, it will "rain" inside the model.

 Strategic Tips

1. Although this lesson can be completed in two sessions, children enjoy this activity so much that you may wish to allow extra time to repeat it.

2. With younger children, you may wish to limit the geographic features to a number you feel they can handle comfortably.

3. You may have the children create their own glossaries, complete with their own definitions and illustrations, after using the data sheet.

Exploring Shapes on the Earth's Crust

e a r t h

Color and write the name that fits the definition:

1. Land surrounded by water on 3 sides is a _____.

2. A _____ is pointed land that sticks out into water.

3. Peninsulas or capes create protected bodies water called

   _____ or _____.

4. Flat land is a _____.

5. Land surrounded by water is an _____.

6. Water surrounded by land is a _____.

7. Folded land can create _____.

8. Water flowing through a bed is a _____.

9. Continents gently slope down. First is the continental

   (a) _____ which slopes deeper under water to

   the continental (b) _____.

   continent

10. The deepest part of the ocean

    is called a (c) _____.

11. There are even (d) _____ under the ocean!

Shadow Play

Shadow Play is *recommended for Grades 1–4*

Lesson Overview

Flashlights, clay, and a popsicle stick make it easy to recreate the Earth's movements in an activity designed to help children realize that shadows change direction and size during the day, leading to the discovery of these . . .

Science Principles

1. Events take time to occur.
2. An event may happen in a repetitive pattern or sequence, making it predictable.
3. Position and movement in space are relative to the observer.
4. Time is measured from one event to another.

Materials Needed

For each group
1. A flashlight.
2. A small lump of clay or plasticine.
3. A popsicle stick.

For each child
4. Data sheet.

Getting Started

1. Ask the children if anyone has ever played the game called "Shadow Tag." Have someone describe how the person who is "it" must tag the shadow on the ground.

   Have the children visualize being "it." Is there a particular time of day they would not want to play? Most children will realize that night would be a terrible time to play due to the lack of sunlight.

   If it is easier to tag someone's shadow when it is longer, what would be the best time of day to play the game?

   Write MORNING NOON AFTERNOON on the board and allow the children to vote. They may vote for two of the choices, if they wish. Record the number of votes, and inform the children that they are going to perform an experiment to find out if their vote was a correct prediction.

   Inform them that they will also find out how to use the sun and shadows to help find their way and tell time.

Procedure

1. Darken your room so that you can still see the data sheet but shadows become distinct.
2. If your children have not had experiences creating shadows, be sure to allow several minutes for shadow play using hands and flashlights.

   Elicit that a shadow is made when an object blocks light, and light outlines the shape of the object. Invite the children to try to make their hand shadows bigger or smaller by experimenting with the position of their hands and of the light source.

3. Have the children place the lump of clay on the labeled spot on the data sheet. They should then insert the popsicle stick in the clay so that it stands upright.

4. Have one child in the group stand up and hold the flashlight so it shines directly down upon the data sheet from 20–30 cm above.

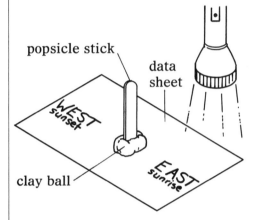

6. Another child positions the data sheet so the light is shining directly upon the word EAST (where there is also the number 1). Be sure the children notice the word SUNRISE, as well.

   All children should observe where the shadow points (to the west) and whether it is long or short (long).

7. The child should then move the sheet in a horizontal line so that its center approaches the stationary light very gradually.

   This will permit the children to see the shadow change by shrinking in size. The sheet should be stopped when the flashlight is directly overhead in the NOON position.

   The children should then note their observation of the shadow, and perceive that at noon the shadow is so short as to be virtually nonexistent. Indeed, if the flashlight is lined up directly over the stick figure, the shadow will disappear. (A child outside

would, in effect, be standing on his or her own shadow. Though this is completely true only in the tropics, it is almost true elsewhere.)

   Ask the children how the position of the number 12 on a clock can help them remember where shadows are during the day.

8. The child should continue to move the paper gradually, until the section labeled WEST is directly under the "sun."

   The children should notice that the shadow grows longer as the stick moves away from being directly under the sun, and that the shadow is now pointing in the opposite direction, toward EAST.

9. After recording the observations, the children should be able to state when they would never play shadow tag (at noon), and what two times would be best (morning and afternoon).

10. Ask how a driver could tell if she was traveling east or west, if she knew what time it was. (Look either at the position of the sun or at the position of the shadows. The shadows would point east during the afternoon, when the sun is in the west.)

    Ask what time a driver could *not* tell directions from the sun. (Noon, just like in shadow tag.)

11. The children will want to know how to find north and south. Explain that if they face east, they should point their left hand out to the side to find north. What direction would their right hand then point to?

e a r t h

Shadow Play

▲ **PROBLEM:** Why do shadows change during the day?

■ **HYPOTHESIS:** I think shadows change because _____

● **METHOD:**

1. Slowly move the paper (Earth) from EAST following the arrow.

2. Don't move the flashlight (sun).

3. Watch the stick's (child's) shadow.

---

③
WEST
Afternoon
(Sunset)

②
Place Clay
Here
(Noon)

①
EAST
Morning
(Sunrise)

👁 **OBSERVATION:**

1. At sunrise, the sun is in the _____.

   The shadow points _____ and is _____.

2. At noon, the sun is _____ and the shadow _____.

3. At sunset, the sun is in the _____.

   The shadow is _____ and points _____.

★ **CONCLUSION:**

1. Shadows change during the day because the Earth _____.

2. The sun and shadows can help us know the _____ of N, S, E, and W.

The Man in the Moon
Why We Don't Need a Meteorite Umbrella

The Man In The Moon is *recommended for Grades 1–4*

Why We Don't Need A Meteorite Umbrella is *recommended for Grades 2–4*

 Lesson Overview

Classroom astronomers will bombard "model moons" with marble and aluminum foil meteorites to simulate the formation of craters and the "Man in the Moon." They will also realize that the moon's lack of atmosphere and life allowed those craters to remain visible far longer than Earth's craters, and discover these . . .

 Science Principles

1. All matter exerts a gravitational pull toward its center of gravity.
2. Energy can exist within matter as potential energy of movement.
3. Environmental conditions can affect other environmental conditions.

 Materials Needed

1. A poster of the solar system, if possible.
2. A poster of a suited-up astronaut, if possible.

For each group
3. An aluminum foil loaf pan.
4. Flour to fill the pan halfway up.
5. Two marbles.
6. Two balls of aluminum foil equal in size to the marbles.

For each child
7. Data sheet.

 Getting Started

1. Explain that you are going to talk about the oldest "man" in the universe. Ask if anyone has ever noticed him while gazing at the full moon.

    Does anyone know who he is and how he got there? Encourage discussion, and then explain that the impression of his face comes from lunar landscape features such as flat plains called *seas* (which are darker) and pits called *craters* (which are lighter).

    Ask if anyone knows how the craters got there, and why, if the man in the moon is so old, he hasn't changed his appearance in over a billion years.

2. Explain that the children are going to use a model moon made with flour to represent the thick layer of lunar dust. With this model they will understand how the craters, which help to make the face, got there.

3. To make sure everyone knows that gravity is a force which pulls objects to the center of mass, tell the children to stand up.

    Ask them to raise their hands if they think they are good listeners. (They will all do so!) Then tell them to jump up when you count to three.

    Of course, they will come down again. Pretend to be perturbed that they didn't listen, since you explicitly told them only to jump up. Very young children will want to repeat this activity. Elicit a definition of gravity after this experience.

4. Inform the children that while they perform their crater experiments they will also be proving that the moon has gravity. (Many children believe that only the Earth has gravity.)

1 2 3 Procedure

1. Explain that the solar system was formed after a star exploded and threw out a great deal of "space junk." Later most of this material came together again to form our star called the Sun. Some of the larger bits of space junk became planets and asteroids, while smaller bits became comets located way, way out, past the last planet, Pluto.

   Display the poster of the solar system, or draw the planets in orbit around the sun. Be sure to point out the asteroids in their belt between Mars and Jupiter.

   Elicit the fact that the planets are not usually lined up with each other (side by side) in their orbits.

2. Ask if anyone has ever played tug of war. Explain that sometimes some planets catch up with each other and appear to orbit side by side. They then play "tug of war" using gravity instead of a rope.

   This lineup is called *syzygy*, and children love hearing and seeing this uniquely spelled word. Challenge them to spell it before you write the correct spelling on the board.

   Explain that the gravitational power of the planets in syzygy gets added together, like $1 + 1 + 1 = 3$. This added sum of gravity sometimes pulls a hunk

of space junk, such as a comet, from far away so that it starts traveling through the solar system.

3. You may wish to have a role-play in which first one child is a planet trying to move you, and then three children hold hands and try to move you with their combined strength. (Only do this if you are bigger and reasonably confident that one child alone cannot shift you!)

4. The pieces of space junk, which are called *meteors*, come in two kinds. One kind of meteor is very heavy, because it has lots of iron in it, while the other kind is made of a stony material, which is not as heavy.

   Ask: *What would happen to a planet or a moon that was in the path of a rapidly moving meteor?* Have the children write their hypothesis on the data sheet.

   Explain that after a meteor hits a planet or moon (and comes to a stop) it is called a *meteorite*.

5. Have the children carefully heft and compare the weight of the marble and aluminum foil balls. Challenge them to explain what these are going to be models of.

   Ask: *Will the stony meteorite (aluminum foil ball) hit the moon with the same force as the iron meteorite (marble)?*

6. Each child will release a "meteorite" over the moon surface from a height of 30 cm. They will leave the meteorites in place so they can compare the depth of the craters and the depth to which the meteorites sink into the surface.

   The marbles will wreak more havoc upon the "moon" than the foil balls. Expect lots of flour dust to be ejected or scattered upon the table. Tell the kids not to worry about it because this is exactly what happened on the moon. When meteorites hit, dust was thrown up and then settled back upon the surface, creating ray-like designs around the craters.

Ask the children how they can tell that there is gravity on Earth by looking at the flour on the table. Now, how does this *ejecta* from a moon crater prove that the moon also has gravity?

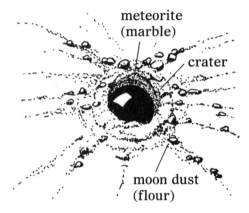

meteorite (marble)

crater

moon dust (flour)

7. At this point, someone is bound to bring up the fact that the Earth must have also been hit by meteorites. Assure them that it was, but ask why the craters which formed are not as visible as the moon's craters.

Ask the children why astronauts have to wear helmets on the moon. (If you have a picture of one, that's great.) Elicit the fact that there is no atmosphere on the moon.

Appoint a child in each group to simulate wind and gently blow on the flour's surface. Ask what has happened to the crater. (The children should notice some erosion.)

Elicit the fact that the Earth's atmosphere with its rain and wind has eroded craters so that most are no longer visible. (Over 200 craters have been found on Earth, but the Earth has been hit many more times than that.)

Ask: *What might grow over and hide craters?* (Plant life)

8. Have the children complete the conclusion. (Answers: 1. meteorites hit its surface; 2. erosion.) Reassure them that the moon's craters formed billions of years ago when there was more space junk flying about than there is today. When they do their homework (see the followup procedure below), they'll find another reason not to worry about being hit by a meteorite.

Meteorites

1 2 3 Procedure

1. Review the top half of the sheet, making sure the children understand that they can find the answers to most of the cloze sentences from the diagram. You may wish to remind the children of what they learned in Air: A Weighty Topic, and also explain the three names of meteors.

Have the children complete this section either in cooperative groups or independently. Acceptable answers: 1. gravity; 2. atmosphere; 3. atmosphere; 4. meteor; 5. meteoroids; 6. meteorites; 7. craters.

Share and go over the answers before assigning the children to do the problem for homework. Analyze vocabulary by looking at the variations of the word *meteor* and its suffixes.

2. When you review the homework after its completion, you might ask if anyone now knows what shooting stars are. (Tiny meteoroids, composed mostly of the leftover tails of comets, burning up as they travel through Earth's atmosphere.) Possible answers: 1. burned up; 2. grew over, hid.

The Man in the Moon

e a r t h

▲ **PROBLEM:** How did the moon get its craters, and why doesn't Earth have as many?

■ **HYPOTHESIS:** _____

● **METHOD:**

1. Heft a marble and an aluminum foil ball. Compare their weight.

2. Drop the "iron meteorite" on the moon from a height of 30 cm.

3. Do the same, using the "stony meteorite."

4. Blow on the "Earth's" surface.

👁 **OBSERVATION:**

1. The heavier meteorite is the

   _____, so I predict

   it will make a _____
   when I drop it.

2. The flour's surface now

   _____.

3. The flour's surface now

   _____.

4. The craters _____.

★ **CONCLUSION:**

1. The moon got its craters when _____.

2. The Earth's craters disappeared due to _____.

Why We Don't Need a Meteorite Umbrella

e a r t h

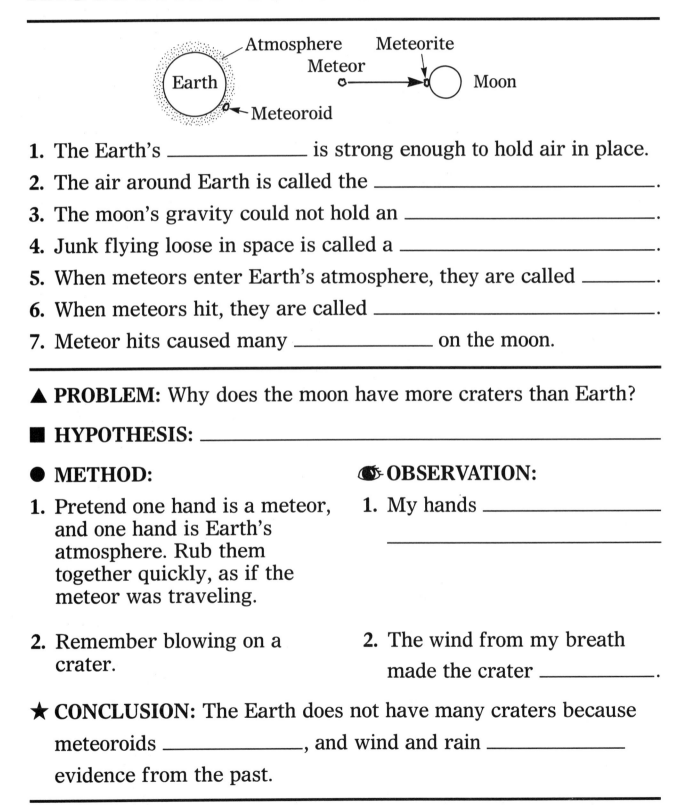

1. The Earth's _____ is strong enough to hold air in place.

2. The air around Earth is called the _____.

3. The moon's gravity could not hold an _____.

4. Junk flying loose in space is called a _____.

5. When meteors enter Earth's atmosphere, they are called _____.

6. When meteors hit, they are called _____.

7. Meteor hits caused many _____ on the moon.

▲ **PROBLEM:** Why does the moon have more craters than Earth?

■ **HYPOTHESIS:** _____

● **METHOD:**

1. Pretend one hand is a meteor, and one hand is Earth's atmosphere. Rub them together quickly, as if the meteor was traveling.

2. Remember blowing on a crater.

👁 **OBSERVATION:**

1. My hands _____ _____

2. The wind from my breath made the crater _____.

★ **CONCLUSION:** The Earth does not have many craters because meteoroids _____, and wind and rain _____ evidence from the past.

What Puts the "System" in Solar?

Birthday Mission (followup)

What Puts the "System" in Solar? *is recommended for Grades 2–4*

Birthday Mission is *recommended for Grades 1 and 2*

Lesson Overview

Why the planets revolve around the sun is simply explained by a ball on a string and some vivid imagination, as your astronomers discover these . . .

Science Principles

1. A system happens when two or more objects interact.
2. An object in motion tends to remain in motion, unless acted upon by another force.

Materials Needed

1. A poster of the solar system.
2. Strong adhesive tape.

For each group
2. A tennis ball.
3. 60 cm of yarn or string.

Getting Started

1. Before class, securely tape one end of each string to each tennis ball, and tie a two-inch loop at the other end of the string.
2. Show the children the poster or drawing of the solar system and have them recount the theory of how the solar system began. Ask them to imagine the massive ex-

plosion and spewing out of star matter into space.

Elicit that the matter became the planets which orbit or revolve around the exploded star which eventually became our sun.

3. Explain that they are going to discover how a mysterious, invisible force acts like glue to hold the planets and sun together in a system.

1 2 3 Procedure

1. Clear an area in the room with a radius of 10 feet. Call up a child volunteer to go on a space mission which happened 4½ billion years ago.

   Ask the children to imagine that you are the exploding star that became the sun, and that the child is some of the matter that spewed from the explosion.

   Bring the child near you, hold hands firmly and have the children count down, 3–2–1 BOOM! At the boom, the child is to try to run away from you, the exploding star.

   Don't let go, and the child will begin to swing around you in a partial orbit. Keep it up, if you have the strength, and the child will swing in a complete revolution.

2. Ask: *Does anyone know what the runaway child was supposed to be?*

   (A planet.) *How about my arm which pulled the child back?* (Don't be upset if no one realizes yet that the arm represents gravity.)

3. Show the children the ball with the string attached. Explain that one child is to slip a finger in the loop of the string and then place the fingertip on the floor.

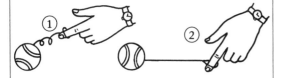

Another child is to take the ball and place it near the child's finger. Then their group goes 3–2–1 BOOM, and the child holding the ball is to roll it away from the finger as fast as possible.

The observation should note that the ball first travels in a straight line but then begins to travel in an orbit along the floor.

4. Have the children remove the string. Now another child is to act as the exploding sun. When the group says 3–2–1 BOOM, this child is to roll the ball away from him or her.

Of course, the ball will continue to roll away in a straight line until it collides with something or friction stops it, the way a planet would if the sun did not have enough gravity to stop it.

5. Ask if anyone knows why the ball did not roll in a circle as it did before. The children will realize that the string extending from their finger kept the ball from escaping.

6. Before the conclusion is reached, have the children stand and jump up. Ask why they came down, and if anyone now knows what invisible force the string and your arm represented.

7. Gravity is the invisible "glue" which holds the system together, and without the sun's gravity the planets would have gone flying off into space until they collided with another object.

The *revolution* or *orbit* is the compromise between the planets' movement to escape and the sun's gravity pulling them back.

Make sure the children understand the connection between *revolve* and *revolution* (revolving). To reinforce the idea that orbit and revolution are synonymous, have the children recall walking about in an orbit through a revolving door.

8. To check for understanding, ask if anyone now knows why the moon orbits the Earth. (The Earth's gravity prevents the escape of the moon from its path.)

Conclusion answers: 1. gravity; 2. orbit, revolution.

Birthday Mission

Procedure

1. Ask the children if they know how many orbits or revolutions around the sun they have taken.

Call up 12 children and have them form a circle. Place a globe in one child's hand and tell him/her to pass it to a neighbor after the class says the month *January*. Each time a month is said, the globe is to be passed to the next child.

2. Before the globe gets passed, ask for a prediction of where the Earth will be after *December* is spoken.

Solar System: What Makes It a Real System?

earth

▲ **PROBLEM:** What force hold the solar system together?

■ **HYPOTHESIS:** The parts of the solar system, such as the

_____ and the _____, are held together by

_____.

● **METHOD:**

1. Place a finger in the loop of string. Keep the ball near your finger. Have a friend quickly roll the ball away from your finger. How does the ball travel *at first*?

2. When the ball reaches the end of the string, what happens?

3. Remove the string. Roll the ball. Does it do what it did in **2**?

👁 **OBSERVATION:**

1. At first, the ball travels in a

_____.

2. Then the ball begins to

_____.

3. Now the ball _____

_____.

★ **CONCLUSION:** The string represented the sun's force of

_____, which makes runaway planets travel in a

_____ or _____.

Birthday Mission

earth

Your mission is to take a trip around the sun. You will be traveling on Earth!
Fill in each month, and write your birthday month in a fancy, funny way!

*Start here:

January

A trip around the sun will take us _____ months or _____ year.
Color the sun yellow and the Earth light blue.

As the Earth Spins: Night and Day

Recommended for Grades K–2

Lesson Overview

What causes day and night is simply explained by a ball on a string, a flashlight, a nose, and imagination in a quick lesson, as astronomers discover these . . .

Science Principles

1. A system happens when two or more objects interact.
2. An object in motion tends to remain in motion unless acted upon by another force.

Materials Needed

1. A globe.
2. A small ball of plasticine.
3. A small flag (like a decoration placed on an appetizer).
4. A lantern flashlight, or lamp with shade removed, that you can easily hold.
5. Strong adhesive tape.
6. A marker.

For each group
7. A tennis ball.
8. 60 cm of yarn or string.
9. A flashlight.

For each child
10. Data sheet.

Getting Started

1. Before class, place the ball of plasticine upon the globe, in your location. Place the flag in the ball so it stands up.

    Test the lantern or lamp with different watt bulbs to be sure that it lights only one half of the globe when you hold it to the side of the globe.

    Securely tape one end of each string to each tennis ball, and tie a two inch loop at the other end of the string. Use a marker to place a large dot of color on the ball's "equator."

2. Ask the children what makes the difference between day and night. The children are most likely to answer "sunlight," "darkness," or something else that is not a cause. Say that they will have to go through a lot of days and nights to find the answer—but not to worry, these will be speeded up to fit into one lesson.

Procedure

1. Introduce the concept of rotation by having one child stand and, at your signal, slowly turn about while remaining on the same spot. Explain that her head is the Earth and her nose is where she lives. Have another child hold your flashlight "sun" and aim it at the first child's head.

    The Earth child should slowly rotate and notice when she faces the flashlight sun.

2. To reinforce the concept that the Earth rotates all the while it is orbiting, have the groups use the tennis balls, string, and flashlight.

One child holds the flashlight as the sun. The other child suspends the tennis ball from a finger and twists the ball on the string many times.

The child holding the ball begins to orbit the sun and allow the ball to untwist on the string, thus simulating rotation occurring at the same time as revolution.

Tell the children to notice if the dot on the ball always faces the sun. When the children state that it does so only half of the time, ask what causes day and night—rotation or revolution?

3. Repeat the experiment as a demonstration, using the globe and lamp in a completely darkened room. You hold the lamp while a student holds the globe and slowly spins it.

 Strategic Tips

1. Test for understanding of the positions of the sun and Earth during day and night by having the children complete the bottom half of the data sheet (drawing the sun in the correct position).

2. Tie this lesson to calendars and math by asking questions such as: *How many rotations equal one revolution? How many hours would two rotations take? How many rotations occur in one month?*

As the Earth Spins!

e a r t h

▲ **PROBLEM:** What causes night and day? (Rotation or Revolution?)

■ **HYPOTHESIS:** _____

● **METHOD:**

👁 **OBSERVATION:**

1. Have a friend shine a light on your nose.

1. I see the _____.

2. Rotate (turn around), so you face away. Do you see the light?

2. _____

_____

3. Have a friend hold the "sun." Spin the tennis ball by twisting it on its string and letting go. Does the dot on the ball (Earth) always face the sun?

3. _____

_____

4. Repeat, but now walk around the sun in an orbit (revolution) while the "Earth" also rotates.

4. _____

_____

★ **CONCLUSION:** The motion of the Earth that causes night and

day is _____.

Draw where the sun must be:

Earth

physical

Float or Sink?

Recommended for Grades K–4

Lesson Overview

The littlest landlubbers will predict and discover which objects float or sink as they discover these . . .

Science Principles

1. Objects sink or float due to certain physical properties they possess.
2. Two objects cannot be in the same place at the same time. Therefore objects which sink displace the water into which they have been placed. Objects which float displace the water in part.
3. When objects are placed in a container of water, displacement makes the water level rise, although the amount of water in the container remains the same.

Materials Needed

1. A permanent marker
2. A small piece of paper (1 square cm).
3. A tall, clear cylinder container (as large as you can get)
4. Several balls of clay with diameters smaller than the diameter of the cylinder.

For each group of two

5. One 10-ounce clear plastic drinking cup.
6. A pitcher or container of water.
7. A small container of assorted junk such as: marbles, buttons, washers, sponge bits, small wooden blocks, Lego, etc.

For each child

8. Data sheet.

Getting Started

1. Before class, use a permanent marker to draw a line approximately halfway up each plastic cup and your demonstration cylinder.
2. To open the lesson, invite one child to stand on a small (1 square cm) bit of paper. Ask another to stand on *exactly* the same spot at *exactly* the same time. Expect some children to suggest sharing the paper, but remind them that they would not then be in the same spot. Expect someone to suggest taking turns, but then they would not be in the same spot at the same time.

   Establish that it is impossible for two objects to be in the same place at the same time, and that if two cars tried it there would be an accident!

   Note: Although you may have given the children this challenge in Earth Science you will find it well worth repeating.
3. Show the children your tall cylinder half-filled with water. Ask them to predict what will happen to a ball of clay if you place it in the container. Will it sink or float?

   Then ask what will happen to the water.

   Have the children observe the change in water level as you drop the first ball into the cylinder.

Ask if anyone saw you put in more water. Challenge the children to predict what will happen if more balls are added to the container. (The water level will rise.) Then demonstrate with the other balls.

4. Ask if anyone can explain why the water level rose—and what that has to do with two children trying to be in the same place at the same time. (The object displaced the water—or pushed it out of its spot—like two children taking turns on the paper.)

 Procedure

1. The children will work with a partner, first to examine the "junk" objects and then to discuss whether or not these will sink or float if placed in their cups of water.

   Predicted sinkers and floaters can be placed on one child's data sheet placed between the partners.

2. Model the type of discussion you want the partners to hold when predicting sinking and floating ability. "I predict this will sink because it has holes in it" would be a good example of a prediction because it gives a reason (even if the reason may be wrong).

3. The children will fill their cup carefully to the marked line, and then proceed to takes turns with their partners placing objects into the cup.

   All objects should remain in the cup to allow for discussion following the testing procedure.

4. Older children should record the results by noting the objects which sank or floated. It is not necessary for younger children to do so.

5. The children should draw a line on the cup pictured on the bottom of the data sheet to denote the new water level which was created after all the objects were placed into the water.

6. Ask the children to explain why certain objects floated or sank. Elicit physical properties such as "heaviness" or "shape."

   You may wish to ask for another list of properties which have no influence on whether objects can float—smell, color, luster, etc.

7. Ask if anyone can explain why he or she had to draw a new water line on the cup at the bottom of the data sheet.

8. Check for understanding by asking what would happen if the children filled their bathtub up to the very top, and then got in. Then ask: *Why aren't swimming pools filled to the very top? Why can't you put ice cubes into a glass which is filled very high?*

Strategic Tips

1. Have plenty of paper towels around so children can clean up.

2. Have the children sit on their papers during the experiments to protect the papers from water splashes.

3. Have older children research Archimedes' Principle: He discovered that an object weighs less in water because the force of buoyancy offsets the force of gravity acting upon the object.

Float or Sink?

Which objects will **float**?

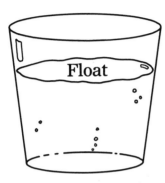

Which objects will sink?

Draw the water line as it appears now.

Before

Now

Playground Physics
Playground Architects
Riding The Coaster (followup)

physical

All Recommended for Grades 2–4

 Lesson Overview

Swinging pendulums will allow your athletes and playground fans to delight in finding that success in sports is related to these . . .

 Science Principles

1. Energy is never created or destroyed but it often changes form. For example, a child perched atop a hill on a sled has gravitational potential energy which will be soon converted into kinetic energy (energy of motion) as the sled begins sliding down the hill.

2. Energy can be stored within an object as potential energy. The position of an object determines the amount of gravitational potential energy which is stored, and which can then be changed into kinetic energy (energy of motion).

3. Energy must be added to a system in order to have that system begin or continue functioning.

4. *Inertia* (the property of a body at rest to remain at rest, or of a moving body to continue moving) and *friction* resulting from parts of a system moving against each other are the reasons energy must be added to a system.

5. Energy can travel through matter or be transferred between objects.

 Materials Needed

1. Masking tape.
2. An oversized tennis racket and a racket with a smaller head (or a racketball racket).

For each group

3. One length of string, such as monofilament fishing line. (The length depends upon the height of the children's desk. See "Getting Started" 1, below)
4. One heavy steel washer (1½ inches wide if possible).
5. Two 30 cm rulers.
6. One wooden block (no bigger than an alphabet block).

   Note: Followup materials are listed in the followup sections.

 Getting Started

1. Before class, set up the pendulums by tying a length of monofilament string to each washer. Tape the other end to the desk top or table top where each group will be working. Be sure that the washer hangs about a centimeter from the floor.

   Note: An uncarpeted floor is best for this activity.

2. Pique the children's interest by waving a tennis racket and saying, "Anyone for tennis?"

   Show the larger racket and the smaller one and ask, *Why do you think people choose to play with the larger racquet? Why do base-ball players get ready to hit by putting their bat all the way back? What do sports have to do with physics? What is physics?* (The science of how matter and energy behave in the physical world.)

Tell the children that after this lesson's physics adventure, they should be able to explain their choice of tennis racket, and why ball players and golfers work so hard on their swing. They will also find out why it's silly to walk in front of the swing set on the playground.

Procedure

1. The swinging washer represents a child on a swing or the raised end of a tennis racket or baseball bat. The small wooden block represents the "blockhead" who walks in front of the swings, or the ball to be hit by the racket or bat.

2. The children will take turns as (a) the swinger (who lets go of the washer), (b) the swing measurer (who uses one ruler to determine the height to which the washer is pulled back), (c) the block measurer (who uses the other ruler to determine the distance the block travels), and (d) the recorder of the information.

3. The children will first make a prediction about the distance the block will travel using energy of motion (kinetic energy) imparted by the washer. Will it travel farther when the washer is released from a height of 5 cm or from a height of 15 cm?

   To help the children hypothesize and predict, remind them of experiences they have had sledding down high hills and low hills. On which did they travel farther? In other words, when did they have more potential energy stored in their bodies waiting to change into kinetic energy—at the top of a high hill or a low hill?

4. The child releasing the pendulum mass should be sure that it is in line with the block so that there is a direct hit.

   This activity provides a good opportunity for discussing how important it is to keep all variables the same except for the one variable being tested (in this case, height).

5. After the children test and record their data at least four times, you may elect to have them throw out the highest and lowest scores. Have them share the data about the distance traveled with the entire class while you record it on the board.

   Depending on math skills, you may elect to average the block travel data with a calculator, or have the children do it themselves.

6. The children should arrive at the conclusion that the higher the object, the more potential energy it has. The potential energy was changed into kinetic energy, which was transferred to the block, which then traveled across the floor.

7. The "Aha! Now I Know" section of the data sheet should help your athletes tie physics to their daily life. They should now know that to hit a ball farther, they should hold the bat or racket back and up. This position allows them to get the most potential energy which can be changed into kinetic energy. In the same way that the swinging washer's energy was transferred into the block, the energy from their body will then be transferred into the ball for a homerun or a sizzling serve.

1. After the experiment, challenge the children to predict what would happen if they had more washers (increased mass) on the string. Would the block travel farther? What implications does this have for automobiles involved in collisions with heavy trucks?

   What if a heavier block were used? Would the block travel as far? Why, or why not?

2. Experiment with placing the block upon a carpeted surface as opposed to a smoother one. Which surface allows the block to travel farther?

3. If you use the two prior suggestions, be sure to ask the children why they shouldn't change the weight of the washer while they also change the surface the block is placed upon.

   They should realize that changing two variables in an experiment will prevent them from knowing which variable is causing changes, and thus they will be unable to draw a valid conclusion.

Playground Architects

 Procedure

1. A wide variety of materials can be used for this activity, such as: popsicle sticks, string, small washers, and small building kits such as Lego.

2. The top section of the data sheet is intended for a quick review of energy and friction.

   Remind the children that as playground designers they must account for the effects of gravity, the height the swings can reach, and how friction will affect their playground equipment.

2. Encourage them to design their own new pieces of equipment rather than merely rearrange standard playground equipment.

3. The purpose of the bird's eye view is to encourage the children to think of the safety areas that must be provided around the equipment when it is moving.

   The use of scale will integrate this activity into your math curriculum. The paragraphs explaining how the forces of inertia and gravity, and the types of energy (kinetic and potential) affect the equipment will require children to write analytically.

Riding the Coaster

 Procedure

1. The top section of the activity sheet provides for a quick review of how energy changes in a roller coaster system.

2. Children may construct three-dimensional coasters using tagboard, with found objects such as empty matchboxes for the coaster's cars.

   Clay balls can be piled one atop another to form the base for the tracks to rest upon. A tagboard track cut in a spiral pattern can then be placed upon the different stacks of balls.

   This is not a working model, but an exciting way to help the children transfer a two-dimensional idea to three dimensions.

3. The children should be aware that the first hill in the system must be the highest, to put the maximum amount of potential energy into the system. In a real coaster, electrical energy is used

only to raise the cars to the top of the first hill. If it were not the highest hill, additional electrical energy would be needed to help the cars get up succeeding hills.

4. To create a working model, some of my students have constructed coasters using aluminum wire for the track and washers for the cars. The object is to have the washer run continuously down the wire from start to finish.

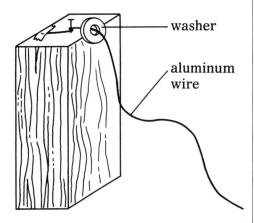

In a coaster of this type, there is too much friction for the washers to store enough potential energy to coast up steep hills. Your designers will have to experiment with different up and down grades in order to make the washers go the distance.

One note of caution: the ends of the wire can be quite sharp, so be sure to have the students cover them with masking tape.

5. Possible answers to data sheet. 1. motion; 2. motion; 3. stored; a. electrical; b. potential; c. kinetic; d. potential; friction

Playground

physical

▲ **PROBLEM:** Why is it dangerous to be near a "high swinger"?

■ **HYPOTHESIS:** _____

● **METHOD:**

1. Release swing from height of 5 cm. Let it go to strike "blockhead." Measure distance blockhead travels. Repeat 4x.

2. Repeat process—but release from height of 15 cm.

👁 **OBSERVATION:**

1. The blockhead travelled

_____ cm.

_____ cm.

_____ cm.

_____ cm.

_____ cm.

_____ cm.

_____ cm.

_____ cm.

★ **CONCLUSION:** The "high swinger" had more _____

_____ which transferred to the block.

AHA! Now I know why baseball batters put their bats so high—so do golfers! This position allows

them to _____

_____.

Playground Architects!

physical

Physicist's Word Box

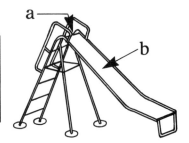

potential energy = stored energy
kinetic energy = motion energy
friction = two objects rub each other

a. At the top of the slide, **a** is waiting with _____ energy.

b. Now, sliding, **b** is using energy of motion—or _____ energy.

c. When a child slows down, there is _____ between the child and the slide.

Now Design a School Playground!

1. Your playground should have at least 3 pieces of equipment on it.

2. You may invent new equipment if you wish.

3. Be sure to leave enough room around the equipment so "blockheads" don't get hurt!

4. Make a "birds eye" view map of the playground.
   Label all equipment pieces.
   Make a scale: For instance 1 ft = 1 cm.
   (That means equipment which takes up 10 feet of room will take up 10 cm. on your drawing.)

5. You may also use cardboard, blocks, clay, etc. to build a 3-D model.

6. Write and attach a paragraph explaining how friction and inertia affect the equipment.

7. List the motions children use on the equipment.

Riding the Coaster (followup)

1. Kinetic energy is energy of _____.

2. Mechanical energy is also energy of _____.

3. Potential energy is _____ energy.

A Roller Coaster is an example of a system with many energy changes. First—electrical energy is put in to start the system.

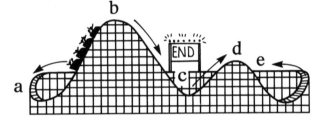

a. A chain powered by _____ energy pulls the coaster up to the top hill.

b. The cars wait at the top ready to come down. Now, the electrical energy is stored as _____.

c. Moving through point **c,** they have _____ energy.

d. At **d,** the cars again have _____ energy.

e. The cars are slowing down, as the coaster system loses energy due to _____.

Now, Design a Coaster!

1. Create a coaster using paper, tagboard, tape, glue and/or clay.
2. Label the energy changes that will occur.
3. Explain how inertia and friction affect your roller coaster system.

Sound—An Energetic Experience!

physical

Recommended for Grades K–4

 Lesson Overview

Through a cacophony of child created "musical" instruments and some simple experiments, your physicists will "feel and hear" these . . .

 Science Principles

1. Sound is a form of energy which occurs when vibrations pass through matter and are sensed.
2. Low pitched sounds occur when longer, thicker pieces of matter vibrate slowly. Conversely, high pitched sounds occur when shorter, thinner pieces of matter vibrate quickly.

 Materials Needed

1. A ball of string.
2. A ruler.
3. A test-tube rack with tubes, or half a dozen soda bottles (optional).

For each group

4. A tuning fork. (If you cannot obtain enough for each group, use one tuning fork to demonstrate the activities.)
5. A container of water. (A clear shoebox is fine.)

For each child

6. One popsicle stick.
7. Data sheet.
8. Eight wooden splints or coffee stirrers.

9. Two tongue depressors.
10. White glue.
11. Scissors.
12. Markers.
13. 3 feet of yarn.

Optional

14. One paper towel or toilet paper tube (core).
15. One square of wax paper (large enough to fit over the end of the paper tube).
16. One rubber band.
17. One straw.
18. One Q-tip.

 Getting Started

1. Before class begins, tie one end of a 3 or 4 foot string to one leg of each table near where each group will sit. Also, tie a string to the door knob near your setup table at the front of the room.
2. Ask what sound is. Can we see it, feel it? To help establish that sound is a form of energy which occurs when an object vibrates at a speed our ears can detect, show the children the string tied to the door. Hold the loose end of it and pull it taut. Pluck it. Do this several times, and elicit that the string moves back and forth in a vibrating pattern whenever a sound is produced.

   Show the children a ruler and ask how they can use it to make a sound. With the ruler projecting over the edge of the table, hold it firmly in place with one hand while pushing and releasing the free end to create vibrations and sound.

3. Distribute popsicle sticks and challenge the children to get the sticks to make a sound by vibrating, the way the ruler did. (**Caution them not to "launch" the sticks.**)

   Challenge the children to discover how to change the sound of the stick. They can do this two ways, by changing the loudness (amplitude) and the pitch.

   Demonstrate with your ruler. First snap the ruler with less force to make the sound softer. Then slide more of the ruler onto the table so that the vibrating section is shorter and the sound is pitched higher.

4. Elicit that sound is created only when vibrations occur by inviting the children to take turns getting the strings to vibrate by plucking them. Challenge them to change the pitch. (By shortening the amount of the string that can vibrate.)

5. Model how to use a tuning fork by showing how to hold it by the handle and strike the side of the fork against the table or desk edge. Ask the children what they notice the tuning fork doing.

   In addition to the sound, guide them to notice the blurry appearance of the fork as it vibrates. They should also notice that the tuning fork makes no sound when it does not look blurry.

Procedure

1. Ask the children to predict what will happen if they touch the surface of the water with the vibrating fork. After they write their predictions, invite them to take turns trying the method.

2. For the conclusion, elicit that the vibrating tuning fork was able to move the water. Therefore, the sound coming from the fork was a form of energy.

3. Discuss how the children's hands felt when they held a sound producing tuning fork. Could they feel the vibrations travel into their hands?

4. Challenge the children to devise a way to have one tuning fork make another tuning fork produce a sound without banging it. (They should be able to touch one vibrating fork prong to a silent one and make the latter start.)

5. You may wish to end this session by having the children construct some instruments. One may be called a stick lyre or African thumb piano.

   The children create a stick lyre by gluing the ends of eight wooden splints between two pop sticks. After the glue has set, the children can use scissors to cut the splints into varying lengths, so they resemble a staircase. You may wish to have the children decorate the splints with markers. Then they can tie yarn at each end of the popsicle sticks, so they can wear the lyre around their necks.

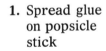

1. Spread glue on popsicle stick

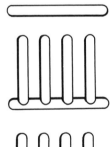

2. Place 4–8 splints on top of glue

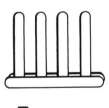

3. Spread glue on second popsicle stick and place over splint ends

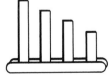

4. Trim splints to varied stepped lengths

6. An alternative instrument is a kazoo. First have the children hum a tune through their toilet paper tube while holding their hand near the end of it. What do they feel? Can they feel the sound traveling through air?

Ask: *What do you think will happen if you put some waxed paper on the end of the tube and then sing through the tube?* Have the children place a square of waxed paper on the end of the tube and secure it with a rubber band. Then they should poke a hole in one side of the tube near mouthpiece.

Have them hum or sing through the tube again. *What do you observe about the waxed paper?* (Vibrations) Allow time for the children to decorate and write their names on the tube.

7. Another, very simple instrument can be made by inserting a Q-tip into one end of a straw. The children then blow across the other end while sliding the Q-tip up and down to vary the pitch. (Caution the children not to walk around as they play.)

 Strategic Tips

1. As a followup, use test tube racks and test tubes, or soda bottles, to have the children create mouth organs. After filling each test tube with a different level of water, they can blow across the tubes quickly, back and forth.

Sound . . . An Energetic Experience!

physical

▲ **PROBLEM:** Can sound make water move?

■ **PREDICTION:** _____

● **METHOD:**

1. Hold the tuning fork by the handle. Gently strike it against the side of the table.

2. Gently strike the fork again. Barely touch the water's surface with the vibrating fork.

👁 **OBSERVATION:**

1. My hand feels _____

   _____

   while I hear the fork.

2. The water _____

   _____

   _____

★ **CONCLUSION:** When the vibrating fork touched the water, the water _____.

This means that sound is a form of

_____ because it had the

power to move the water.

Sound Science

physical

Recommended for Grades K–4

 Lesson Overview

Use this lesson after An Energetic Experience and your scientists will "chime" right in to discover these . . .

 Science Principles

1. Sound is a form of energy which varies in its ability to move through different mediums.
2. Sound travels in all directions and spreads out around corners.
3. Sound energy really is energy of motion which must pass through matter in order to be received by our ears.
4. Sound travels more efficiently through solids than liquids or gases. Because the molecules in solids are packed more closely together than those in other states of matter, they pass motion energy (vibrations) more quickly from one to another.

Materials Needed

1. A ball of string.

For each group (optional)

2. A container of water, such as a clear shoebox.
3. A tuning fork.

For each child

4. A metal hanger.
5. Data sheets and followup sheet.

 Getting Started

1. Before class, tie a 2 or 3 foot length of string to a leg of the table for each student.

   Also tie 40 cm of string to each end of each student's hanger.

2. Remind the children that they cannot see behind them because light does not travel around corners. How does sound travel?

   Call up a volunteer to perform the following demonstration: Have the child close his/her eyes. Then snap your fingers in various positions around his/her body and have the child determine where the sound is coming from.

   If the child can hear the sound coming from positions away from his/her ears, that proves that the sound travels in all directions. Also, the rest of the class can still hear the finger snaps when they come from behind the child's body.

   Ask for evidence in real life to further prove this. (Ambulances can be heard from the next street, music travels from one room to all parts of the house, the children can hear your voice when you are writing on the board, etc.)

3. Have the children work with a partner to try the finger snapping test (or tap a ruler with a pencil).

4. You may wish to have the children test the tuning forks in water again to observe how the resulting wave travels in all directions.

5. Have the children note their hypothesis in answer to the first question on the data sheet.

 Procedure

1. The instructions for the first step in the method state that the children place their heads on the table and close their eyes while the teacher knocks on one section of the table top. (If the children do not share common tables, have several children place their heads on a common desk.)

   Knock very softly so the sound cannot be heard unless their heads are placed upon the table.

2. Ask the children to lift their heads up and raise their hands if they heard the knock.

3. Since the sound of the knock traveled to everyone's ear from the one spot where you knocked, the children should realize that sound does travel in all directions. Conclusion answers: in all directions, I (everyone at my table) heard the knock.

4. Ask: *What does sound travel through to get to your ears?* Elicit the response, air. Ask the children if they think sound can also travel through solid matter. (Some of your more capable students may realize that the table, which is a solid, carried the knocking sound very efficiently

to their ears. This is a good basis for their hypothesis.)
Then ask: *Which kind of matter is best for carrying sound—air, a gas, or string, a solid?*

5. Instruct the children to complete their prediction on sheet 2, and to write a reason for their prediction, if they wish.

6. Have the children wrap the strings on the hanger gently around their index fingers. They should stand up let the hanger swing gently to tap the edge of their desks, taking care not to let the hangers touch their body and dampen the sound.

   Their observation of how the hanger sounded should be noted with words such as "not too loud," "gentle sound."

   Holding the strings as before, they should now place their fingers in their ears and bang gently, with the same amount of force as before, on the table.

   Encourage the children to write observation 2 with "poetic license." Many children comment excitedly that the hangers now sound just like chimes. Encourage them to include a comparison to the first written observation.

   Ask them which way the vibrations traveled more clearly or loudly—through the air or through the solid string?

7. Before the children write the conclusion, have four of them

come up to act as model air molecules. Have them line up facing the class with several feet of space between them.

You say the magic word "vibration" and the first "molecule" nearest to you will begin to vibrate (shimmy in place) and then slide over to pass the vibration over to the next "molecule," and so on until the vibration has passed to the last child.

Repeat the demonstration, but this time have the children model molecules in a solid by standing shoulder to shoulder. Obviously, when the first child starts to shimmy, the second child will feel the vibration, start vibrating, and pass it to the next molecule a lot faster than when they were standing several feet apart.

8. Have the children note their conclusions. (Cloze answers: a solid; solid's.) Then check for understanding by asking why native Americans would place their ear to the ground when they were hunting buffalo. (They could hear the hooves through the ground before hearing them through the air.)

 Strategic Tips

1. As a followup, challenge the children to get the strings previously tied to the desk legs to make a sound. (They should realize that by placing their ears upon the table while plucking, they will hear the sounds much louder.) Allow time for experimentation.

Physicist _____

Sound Science 1

▲ **PROBLEM:** Does sound travel in one straight line, or does it spread out in all directions? (Will I hear the knock if the teacher doesn't knock near me?)

■ **HYPOTHESIS:** I think sound travels in

_____.

● **METHOD:**

1. Place your head and ear against the table. Close your eyes while your teacher knocks on the table. Did everyone hear the knock?

👁 **OBSERVATION:**

1. _____
could hear the knock.

★ **CONCLUSION:** Sound travels _____

_____. I know this because

_____.

Good... the train will be here soon!

To think about: How does the cowboy know the train is coming?

See the Light

Recommended for Grades 2–4. Can be modified for Grades K–1

Lesson Overview

Your students will "see" that light is the form of energy we need in order to see, and that light energy can also be very surprising, as they discover many of its properties in these . . .

Science Principles

1. Light travels in a straight path through space.

2. Light is perceived only when it reaches the eye either directly from a light source or indirectly, by being bounced off matter which has not absorbed all of its energy.

   Note: A black hole in space must look black because it absorbs all light energy.

3. Light energy can travel through some matter, depending upon the properties of that matter. For example, light travels more easily through matter such as glass than through paper.

4. When a maximum amount of light travels through matter, that matter is classified as *transparent*. When less light travels through, the matter is classified as *translucent*. When no light appears to travel through, that matter is referred to as *opaque*.

5. The thicker the matter, the more difficult it is for light energy to travel through it, even if the matter is normally classified as transparent. For example, although water is transparent in thin layers, light cannot travel very far down through the ocean or a deep lake.

6. The amount of light energy coming from a source determines the brightness of light in an area, and its ability to pass through matter.

Materials Needed

1. A film strip projector (If unobtainable, use a flashlight.)

2. Two very chalky erasers.

3. A hand mirror.

For each group of two

4. Two 10 × 10 cm squares of aluminum foil.

5. Two 10 × 10 cm squares of waxed paper.

6. Two 10 × 10 cm squares of black construction paper.

7. A flashlight. (Ask children to bring one from home if you do not have a classroom supply.)

8. One small pane of glass or clear plastic. (I use new plastic petri dishes, which are cheap and unbreakable.)

For each child

9. Data sheets.

Getting Started

1. Ask the children to imagine they are in a room with no light. Could they read a book? Elicit that it is necessary that light be present before we can see.

2. Turn the lights in the room on and off several times. Ask the children to notice if they have more room around them either way, to establish that light does not take up space. Acknowledge that flashlights and projectors take up space because they are considered matter, but the light emanating from them doesn't take up space.

Therefore light is classified as energy. Today the children will experiment to see how light energy behaves and how its properties affect us.

①②③ Procedure

1. To demonstrate that light travels in a straight line, turn off the lights in the room and use a film strip projector or a flashlight to project a beam of light.

Have the children notice that the light does not illuminate the entire room but only travels across to the opposite wall.

2. To establish that light energy itself is invisible unless transmitted or reflected to the eye, clap two erasers to create dust in the beam of light energy. The children will realize that they could not see the beam until the dust reflected its light to their eyes. They can also see that the beam is relatively straight.

This is an extremely dramatic demonstration that my students usually beg to see over and over again.

Have them complete the first data sheet. Conclusion answers: invisible; in a straight line. "Aha! Now I Know": 1. chalk dust (or anything that reflects light); 2. light cannot travel around furniture and other objects.

3. To demonstrate Reflections on Light (data sheet 2), place the mirror in the projector beam so the children can see the light reflected or bounced onto the back wall. Ask if anyone knows why the light is now on the back wall.

4. The children will discover what makes a mirror able to reflect (bounce) light by using a piece of aluminum foil as a mirror. They will compare how they look in the foil first when it is smooth and then when it is crinkled so the light rays bounce off irregularly.

Have them observe their faces in the smooth foil, and then use a flashlight to bounce the light off the smooth foil onto the ceiling.

They then crumple the foil, open it up, and repeat the same experiments—observing their faces and the amount of light reflected onto the ceiling.

Ask which piece is able to bounce the light straight back to their eyes or to the ceiling—the smooth or wrinkled foil. Ask why mirrors can bounce light so well. Elicit that the smoothness of the metallic paint on the back allows most light to reflect back in a straight path, rather than bounce off irregularly.

5. Distribute a new petri dish to each pair of children, and ask them to look through it at their partner.

Darken the room, and ask for a prediction of what will happen to a light if the petri dish is placed in front of it. Have the children turn on the flashlights, and they will observe the light energy travel through the clear plastic.

Tell them there is a special word for matter that allows light to travel through it—from the words *trans* meaning through and *parent* meaning being seen. Ask: *Can anyone figure out the word that describes clear glass or plastic?*

6. Distribute the waxed paper to each pair of students, and ask them to predict if light can travel through it as well as it did with the plastic dishes.

   Repeat the experiment, and establish that matter which allows some light to travel through it is *translucent*. (*Lucent* means shining.)

7. Repeat the procedure described in steps 3 and 4, using black construction paper. Establish that this matter is *opaque*, because the light did not appear to travel through it all.

   Also have the children feel the rough texture of the paper, to establish that it both scatters and absorbs the light. It is unlike black glass, which can reflect some light because it is smooth.

8. Before the children complete the conclusion, check for understanding of how a mirror works, and the meaning of transparent, translucent, and opaque, by asking if someone can explain why a mirror is made of transparent glass coated on the back with opaque metallic paint. (The clear protective glass allows light to travel through to the metallic paint, which bounces it straight back out to the viewer.)

 Strategic Tips

End of sheet 2

1. Discuss the lists of matter classified as transparent, translucent, and opaque to establish that these properties of matter are very important to take into account when people design buildings, clothing, furniture, and cars.

 Followup

1. In the beam of light demonstration, the beam from the projector or flashlight will spread out slightly, but this is usually not too noticeable if you keep the light source fairly close to the wall.

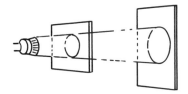

2. To modify this lesson for kindergarten through second grade, cut back on the use of the data sheet and rely more on demonstration. After you model the demonstrations, have the children repeat the experiments for themselves.

   Classify material orally rather than in writing.

3. As a further followup, have the children discover how useful mirrors are by having them practice walking backward through the room, or (in groups) simulate driving in heavy traffic with the help of a rear view mirror.

   Using mirrors in this way will establish the fact the right and left appear reversed. Ask why the word *ambulance* is painted backward on the front of the vehicle.

   Use mirrors in a followup math lesson on symmetry. The children might establish which shapes or letters of the alphabet are symmetrical by placing a mirror on the midline and seeing if the letter is recreated in the mirror. Extend into art, as well, by having the children draw or study symmetrical designs.

4. Ask why lakes or calm oceans change color. The children should realize that the smooth water acts as a mirror to reflect the changing sky.

Physicist _____

See the Light!

▲ **PROBLEM:** Is light energy visible?

■ **HYPOTHESIS:** _____

● **METHOD:**

1. Look at beam of light. Can you see the actual beam?

👁 **OBSERVATION:**

1. I _____ see the actual beam.

★ **CONCLUSION:** Light energy, itself, is _____.

▲ **PROBLEM:** Does light energy travel around corners, or in a straight line?

■ **HYPOTHESIS:** _____

● **METHOD:**

1. Look at beam of light *after* erasers have been clapped.

👁 **OBSERVATION:**

1. The beam of light traveled _____.

★ **CONCLUSION:** Light travels _____.

AHA!

1. Now I know that light can only be seen after it bounces off

something like _____.

2. Now I also know that a big room may need more than one light

source because _____

_____.

Reflections on Light!

physical

▲ **PROBLEM:** How do light energy and matter interact?
OR can matter conduct light energy?
OR can matter bounce light energy?

■ **HYPOTHESIS:** _____

● **METHOD:**

1. Place smooth aluminum foil in beam.

2. Place wrinkled foil in beam.

3. Place clear glass or plastic in beam.

4. Place waxed paper in light beam.

5. Place black construction paper in beam. Feel paper.

👁 **OBSERVATION:**

1. The light _____
_____

2. The light _____

3. The light _____
I can see the _____

4. The light _____
I _____

5. The paper felt _____
The light _____

★ **CONCLUSION:**

1. Matter that blocks and absorbs light is _____.
2. Matter that conducts some light is _____.
3. Matter that conducts light very well is _____.
4. The smoother matter is the more it can _____ light.

★★ **FOLLOW UP:** Make a list of transparent, translucent and opaque objects.

Living in a Greenhouse
Light: Tying It All Together

physical

Both recommended for Grades 2–4

 Lesson Overview

In two or three sessions on sunny days, the link between physical science and life science becomes evident when your physicists discover that light entering a container becomes trapped and turns into heat energy along with these other . . .

 Science Principles

1. Energy can travel through matter.
2. When light energy enters the ecosystem called Earth, it interacts with and changes the physical environment in both positive and negative ways.

   For example, light energy is used for growth and activity when absorbed by the chlorophyll of green plants. However, when solar energy is converted into too much heat energy, the temperatures on Earth can rise and create problems such as melting polar ice caps.
3. White light is composed of different wavelengths and energy levels, which appear to us as different colors of light.
4. Different pigments absorb different amounts of light energy. (This is very difficult for children to understand, since green plants really absorb every color *except* green, bouncing back "green light energy" to our eyes.)

 Materials Needed

1. A globe.
2. One prism (or several, if possible, for the children to handle as well).

For each group

3. Two thermometers. (If you don't have enough, you can conduct this lesson as a demonstration.)
4. Two clear containers (plastic shoeboxes would be fine).
5. One transparent lid or piece of glass to cover one shoebox.
6. Two ice cubes of exactly the same size.
7. Two pieces of construction paper, one black and one white, large enough to place over the thermometers.

For each child

8. Data sheet.

 Getting Started

1. Ask the children if they have ever visited a greenhouse or waited in their car during a sunny day. How did they feel after several minutes had passed?

   Ask if anyone has ever heard of the "greenhouse effect," and inform the children that after today's experiment they will understand what "global warming" is all about.

 Procedure

1. Each group will take readings on both of their thermometers, and

record this base temperature on the data sheet.

2. Have the children predict what will happen if they put one thermometer into a covered box and the other thermometer into an uncovered box, and then place the boxes in the sun.

Will the temperature in each box decrease or increase? Which box will hold on to its temperature longer—the covered box or the uncovered box?

Before the children write their predictions, remind them of how they feel when they sit in a car in the sun.

3. Allow time for the thermometers to register a change, and then have the children record the new temperatures in each box and compute the difference between start and finish.

Encourage the children to brainstorm what form of energy the light energy has changed into, if the temperature has risen. (Heat energy)

Allow several minutes to go by, and record the temperatures again, to see which box has retained the most heat energy.

4. Discuss how the Earth is surrounded by an atmosphere which allows most solar energy in but does not easily let heat energy out.

If the atmosphere gets too thick, like a glass lid placed over the Earth (box), it will trap too much heat energy.

Have the children brainstorm what could thicken the Earth's atmosphere, and they will surely say that pollution can do it. This pollution can take the form of too much carbon dioxide from car exhausts or the burning of any kind of fuel.

Cutting down rain forests increases the amount of carbon dioxide in the atmosphere, because fewer trees are left to use carbon dioxide during the process of photosynthesis. Burning down rain forests is even worse, because these fires add greater amounts of carbon dioxide to the air.

5. Summarize by asking if the children recall what form of energy light changes into when it is trapped in cars, greenhouses, or the atmosphere—and then they will know what "global warming" is all about.

You may wish to end the session at this point.

6. Ask the children to look at the globe and notice if there is any part of the Earth that would be most affected by global warming. If no one comes up with the idea of the polar ice caps, show the ice cubes.

7. Place an ice cube in each container and cover one with the "thickened" atmosphere (lid). Have the children predict what will happen as the containers sit in the sun. Which ice cube will melt first?

8. As the ice cubes melt, have the children brainstorm what would happen to the ocean levels, and the shorelines of continents, if the polar ice caps melted. They will quickly realize that the lives of many people, plants and animals would be jeopardized by rising ocean levels.

Now have the children complete the conclusion. Answers: 1. covered one; 2. heat; 3. pollution (carbon dioxide), heat; 4. warming, melt.

Living in a Greenhouse

▲ **PROBLEM:** Why is it warm in a greenhouse?

■ **HYPOTHESIS:** _____

● **METHOD:**

1. Place the thermometers in 2 containers—one covered, and one uncovered. Record the starting temperature. Place the containers in sunlight.

2. Record the temperatures

   after _____ and _____ minutes.

3. Calculate the difference between the finishing and starting temperatures.

👁 **OBSERVATION:**

(Record on chart.)

	Covered	Uncovered
Starting Temp.		
After ___ min.		
After ___ min.		
Difference in Temp. between start & finish		

★ **CONCLUSION:**

1. The container which gathered the most heat was the _____.

2. Light enters greenhouses through the glass and gets trapped as

   _____ energy.

3. The Earth's atmosphere is getting "thickened" by _____.

   This may trap _____ energy.

4. This can cause global _____ and change the Earth's

   climates. Polar ice caps may _____.

Magnets: An Attractive Science Adventure

Recommended for Grades K–4

 Lesson Overview

In three sessions, your scientists will be forcefully attracted to magnets and their energy as they sort through your "junkyard" to discover these . . .

 Science Principles

1. The properties of an object depend upon what it is made of. For example, a magnet can be made from iron, a metal whose atoms are organized into domains.

2. Domains are like miniature magnets within a magnet. The atoms are arranged so that all of their "south poles" point in one direction and their "north poles" point in the opposite direction.

3. A magnet is created when the domains line up with their south poles pointing in one direction and their north poles pointing in the opposite direction.

4. This means that opposite poles attract each other while like poles repel each other.

5. It also means that if you break a magnet in half, it will become two new magnets, with the appropriate poles.

6. Thus the parts of a magnet that produce the strongest magnetic fields are the poles.

7. The properties of an object can be changed when they interact with another object and a source of energy. For instance, when a permanent magnet comes in contact with another piece of iron or steel (a metal with a high iron content), that object—such as a paper clip—will have its domains rearranged so that they, too, point to a south and north pole.

8. If an object such as a paper clip remains in contact with a magnet for a long enough period of time, the domains in the object will arrange themselves into a temporary magnet.

9. An electric current can also cause domains to align themselves into a magnet.

10. Heating or banging a magnet can cause the domains to become disordered, so that the magnet loses its magnetic field and ability to attract.

 **Materials Needed**

1. A stapler.
2. A pile of household junk—buttons made of metal and plastic, paper clips, aluminum foil, keys, small objects made of steel or iron, ceramic, plastic and wood. (Magnetite, a rock with a high iron content, would be a great addition. It can be ordered inexpensively through science equipment distributors.) There should be

enough items for each child to have about a dozen.

For each group

3. A lunch tray with Yes and No marked on it.

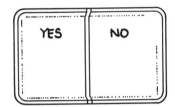

4. A box of paper clips.
5. Four bar magnets of any size, but big enough so that you can mark each end with N and S.
6. A blank sheet of 8 × 11 paper.
7. A sheet of 8 × 11 paper marked N and S.

For each child

8. Data sheets.

 **Getting Started**

1. Before class, mark each lunch tray Yes and No and place 40–50 pieces of junk on it. At this point you may wish to prepare the Yes and No sheets of paper for session three.

    If your magnets are not marked N and S, select one magnet and mark it N and S at its poles. Then take another magnet and see which of its poles is attracted to the N end of the first magnet. Mark that end S. Continue with this marking procedure until all of your magnets are marked.

    When you store your magnets, always align them so the N and S

ends are touching. This will keep them functioning property.

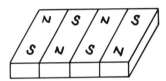

2. Inform the children that you have a mess that needs sorting out. Invite each child to select a number of items off the tray. Depending upon grade level you might instruct them to select 4 × 3 objects or 7 + 4 objects.

    With very young children, have them line their objects up like a train so that they can count more easily.

    Continue to have children select objects until the tray has been cleared, everyone has the same number, and they have noticed the words written upon the tray.

3. Ask the children for ideas on how to sort out the mess. While they are brainstorming, pretend to trip with a container of the paperclips. Ask for ideas on how to clean up the newly created mess, and then whip out a magnet and quickly clear it up.

4. Ask if anyone has noticed the words on the tray, and ask if anyone now has an idea of how to sort out the objects.

 Procedure

1. Elicit that the children are going to place objects that are pulled by the magnet on the side of the tray marked "Yes" and the objects not attracted on the side marked "No."

    Ask if anyone has a general prediction about what an object must be made of in order to be attracted to the magnet. Someone is bound to say, "Metal."

At this time, it is not necessary to clarify that objects made of iron or steel are the only ones going to be attracted. Merely repeat the prediction that metal objects will be attracted.

2. Model how to check by holding an object in your hand and saying, "I predict this will/will not be attracted by the magnet." Then bring the magnet near the object in your hand to see what happens. Ask the children where it should go on the tray.

3. The children will take turns predicting, testing, and placing the objects upon the tray.

4. When all of the objects have been placed, walk around and select some objects from the No side that are made of aluminum or copper or anything else the children would recognize as metal.

   Pretend puzzlement at their placement. Invite a child to explain it, and demonstrate how the magnet could not attract those objects though they were made of metal.

5. Elicit a new statement that only objects made of certain metals will be attracted to magnets. Usually the metals which are attracted to magnets are iron, steel, and nickel.

   If you have magnetite, check for understanding by holding it up and demonstrating how the magnet attracted it. Ask what metal might be hiding in a rock. If you don't have magnetite, hold up any object that was attracted.

   Ask how the class might find out what objects have iron or steel in them in the classroom.

   Caution: If you let children go on an "iron" treasure hunt, be sure to put computers, VCRs, tapes, Nintendos, etc., off limits so they are not damaged by the magnets.

Session Two

6. Remind the children that they know that magnets attract objects made of iron or steel. Inform them that they will now discover something else that magnets do.

7. Ask the children to work with a partner to explore how the magnets react when they are slid near each other's poles. Allow several minutes for this activity, as the children will be delighted to discover the repelling force of the magnets.

8. Discuss the terms *attract* and *repel* by giving examples of favorite foods attracting the children and awful combinations such as ice cream and sardines repelling them.

9. Challenge the children to work with their neighbor to properly label the magnets drawn on the data sheet.

N S	N S
N S	S N
S N	N S

   Then have them complete the conclusion to Problem 1. Answers: 1. attract, attract; 2. repel; 3. repel.

10. Invite the children to hypothesize which part of a magnet has the most energy—the poles or the center.

11. The children will select a pole and hang a paper clip from it. They will then hang another clip from that, and continue doing so until no more clips can be attracted.

    They will then repeat the procedure using the center of the magnet. Caution them that the clips must hang down, not be attracted to the poles.

To record observations, the children will sketch the number of clips hanging from each part of the magnet tested.

12. The children should conclude that the poles have the strongest magnetic force.

Session Three

13. Inform the children that they are going to find out why only certain metals are attracted, and why magnets are able to attract them, by pretending to be atoms—the tiniest building blocks that anything is made of.

14. Distribute a sheet marked N and S to each child. Ask one group to stand up and arrange themselves the way their magnets attracted each other: NS-NS-NS, etc.

Inform the children that they are holding up not magnets but models of what the atoms in iron and steel are like—atoms with ends that act like the poles of a magnet. Their group is now called a *domain.*

Invite another group to form a domain and then join the other domain to create a magnet. You can have the entire class join together to create a huge magnet.

Split the class in half and they will realize why, when magnets are broken, they become two new magnets with the broken ends as the new poles.

17. To have the children understand how magnets pick up paper clips, have one "domain" of children approach a group of "atoms" which are not aligned. The nearest unaligned child should arrange his/her paper so the pole is properly attracted to the magnet. Then the next "atom" should begin to align, until all of the "paper clip atoms" are aligned properly. They will look just like the "magnet atoms" and will have become a temporary magnet, the way their real paper clips did when hung from the magnet.

18. Give blank papers to one group and tell the children they are molecules of plastic. Invite the "domain" over and ask if it can attract the plastic. It will be evident that the plastic can't be aligned because it lacks the easily moved atoms with poles that iron atoms have.

19. Tell the children there is another way to make a paper clip a temporary magnet: stroke it along a permanent magnet.

    Ask them to hypothesize whether more or less stroking will make a paper clip become a magnet.

20. Allow them to proceed to stroke the magnet 50 times with a new paper clip. After every 10 strokes they should try to pick up staples you have discharged from your stapler.

21. Using data sheet 2 (The Attractive Atomic Paper Clip) the children will note the data. They should come to the conclusion that the more the clip strokes the magnet, the more the atoms in it align themselves into domains.

Magnets: An Attractive Science Adventure!

physical

▲ **PROBLEM 1:** What happens when magnets come near each other?

■ **METHOD:** Test by sliding magnets near each other.

👁 **OBSERVATION:** Finish labeling these magnets with N and S.

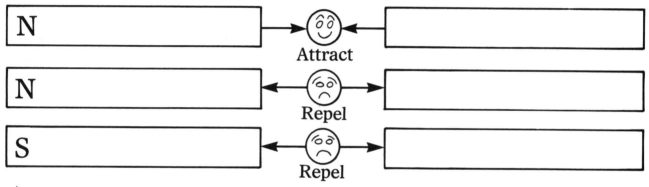

★ **CONCLUSION:**

1. N and S _____. Opposite poles _____.

2. S and S _____.

3. N and N _____.

▲▲ **PROBLEM 2:** What part of a magnet is strongest?

■■ **PREDICTION:** The middle or the poles

👁👁 **OBSERVATION:**

N	S

★★ **CONCLUSION:** The _____ are the strongest because the most clips hung there.

The Attractive "Atomic" Paper Clip

physical

▲ **PROBLEM:** Will more magnet stroking make your temporary magnet stronger?

■ **PREDICTION:** _____

● **METHOD:**

1. Stroke "magnet" paperclip for the number of times shown on the graph. Try to attract staples.

2. Be sure to always use a new paperclip and staples for each trial.

👁 **OBSERVATION:**

1. Record your observations by plotting them on the line graph. Connect the dots when you are finished to find a trend or pattern.

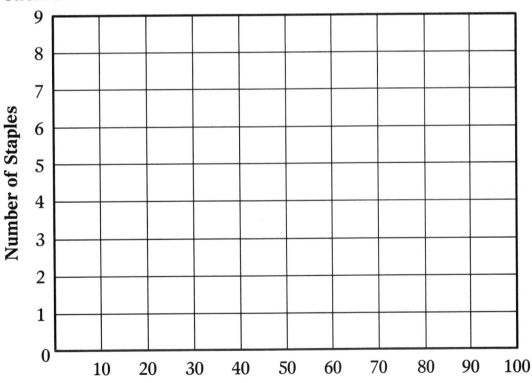

★ **CONCLUSION:** _____

What a Shock!

Lesson Overview

On a day that's not too humid, your children will have an electrifying experience as they try to charge common household items with static electricity and discover these . . .

Science Principles

1. Electrical energy can travel through objects and cause objects to interact with each other.

2. All matter is composed of atoms whose electrons can sometimes be easily removed.

3. When one object has a surplus of electrons and another object has a deficit, the two objects will be attracted to each other because they have opposite charges. These charges are referred to as *positive* and *negative*.

4. If two objects have the same charge they will repel each other. For example, two objects with excess electrons will repel each other because they both have a negative charge.

5. Movement of electrons causes an electrical discharge or current of electricity to occur.

6. Only one variable should be changed at a time during a properly executed experiment.

Materials Needed

1. Two inflated balloons tied together on the same string.

For each child

2. A small plastic comb or half a plastic petri dish. (If you have any of the plastic eggs that pantihose are sometimes packed in, they are terrific for this experiment.)

3. A scrap of fur (either real or synthetic) about 3 × 3 inches. (Ask your colleagues or parents for assistance in obtaining this.)

4. A 3 × 3 inch piece of cotton or felt.

5. 10 puffed wheat or rice cereal bits.

Getting Started

1. Get a volunteer with smooth, unrestrained hair and rub it with a balloon so that it stands on end. After the laughter subsides, explain that by the end of their experiments the children will be able to explain why their friend's hair stood on end.

2. Pretend to walk across the room with a scuffing motion. Touch something metal and yell, "Ouch!"

3. Ask if anyone has ever had an experience like that—and you will elicit a flood of "shocking" stories. Some children will say that static electricity is what caused the shock.

4. Remind the children that matter is made of *atoms*. Explain that atoms are like the building blocks of all matter. Atoms have even tinier building blocks inside them called *electrons* and a central part called the *nucleus*.

Explain that even though an atom is very tiny, we can think of it like the solar system. The nucleus is like the sun and the electrons are like the planets.

Electrons have a minus (negative) charge and the nucleus has the charge opposite to minus—plus (positive).

The electrons are so far from the nucleus that they can easily be stolen away from it. When you scuffed your feet against the floor, electrons were being stolen either from you or from the floor. (The direction in which the electrons move depends on the different materials that rub together.) Then electrons jumped either from you to the knob or from the knob to you, and you felt that discharge of electrons as a little shock.

Remind the children that magnets are attracted to opposite poles and ask what charge they think electrons would be most likely to jump to—the same charge (negative) or the opposite charge (positive)?

Explain that today they will discover what causes objects to become charged with *static electricity*, and they will actually create it. They may find that static electricity can make objects behave in a very surprising way.

1 2 3 Procedure

1. Have the children predict which material will create a larger charge of static electricity—fur, which is fuzzy, or the smoother

pieces of cotton or felt. Have them recall their own experiences with shocks to help them hypothesize.

2. Explain that they will be rubbing a plastic object with the two types of material. Ask if it would be fair to rub the objects for different amounts of time, and they will most likely tell you that both should be rubbed for the same amount of time.

3. Model how to hold the plastic object using your fingertips only. Explain that if you hold the object firmly in your palm, you may end up charging yourself instead of the object.

4. Model how to bring the "charged" object close to the cereal pieces without actually touching them.

5. You can have the children work as cooperative pairs, if you wish, with one child functioning as the "charger" and the other as the timer. After recording the number of pieces of cereal picked up during method step 1, they can switch jobs for step 2.

If no pieces of cereal are picked up (expect that to happen when cotton or felt is used), be sure the children record the number zero.

6. Expect squeals of excitement when the object rubbed with fur makes the cereal jump and cling to the plastic object.

7. Have two "chargers" come up with the material which charged the plastic the most, and invite them to charge the balloons by rubbing them quickly and lightly all over. (They should avoid holding the balloons against themselves while charging.)

Hold the thread at midpoint and allow the balloons to dangle. Of course, if the balloons are charged with the same charge (which they will be, if the children do a good rubbing job) they will fly apart, due to the repelling of like charges.

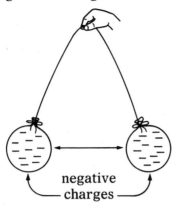

negative charges

8. To check for understanding, repeat the "hair" demonstration and ask for an explanation of why the hair is now standing on end. (The balloon has extra electrons that were stripped away from the hair during the rubbing process, leaving the hair positively charged and making the balloon negatively charged. The hair is now attracted to the balloon the same way the north pole of a magnet is attracted to the south pole.)

Ask for someone to now explain why the cereal jumped onto the plastic objects. Then have the children complete the conclusion. Answers: 1. fuzzy; 2. jump (are stolen); 3. opposite.

 Strategic Tips

1. Work with magnets before this experience. (See Magnets: An Attractive Science Adventure, page 190.)

2. Depending upon the humidity in the air, you may have to increase the amount of seconds for charging during method steps 1 and 2. (If it's very humid, don't even attempt the lesson, because the molecules of water in the air will "steal" the electrons right away.

The best time to conduct static electricity experiments is on a cool, crisp day.)

What a "Shock!"

▲ **PROBLEM:** Which kind of material will make a bigger charge of static electricity?

■ **PREDICTION:** I think the _____ material will make a bigger charge.
(fuzzy or smooth)

● **METHOD:**

1. Rub the smooth fabric on the plastic for 30 seconds. Bring the plastic near the cereal.

2. Rub the fuzzy fabric on plastic for 30 seconds. Bring the plastic near the cereal.

☞ **OBSERVATION:**

1. The plastic attracted _____ pieces of cereal.

2. The plastic attracted _____ pieces of cereal.

★ **CONCLUSION:**

1. The plastic had the biggest charge from

the _____ material.
(fuzzy or smooth)

2. Static electricity happens when electrons

_____ .

3. Electrons jump to the _____
charge.
(same or opposite)

All Aboard!
Electrical Safety Inspector

All Aboard *is recommended for Grades 1–4*

Electrical Safety Inspector *is recommended for Grades K–4 with their parents*

 Lesson Overview

The same junkpile used for your magnetism experiences (page 190) will enable children to construct the simplest of simple circuits, so that they can classify items as conductors or insulators and discover these . . .

 Science Principles

1. Electrical energy moves through an object and from one object to another depending upon the material and composition of the objects.
2. A conductor is a material which allows electrons to flow, while an insulator does not permit electrons to flow freely. Metals are classified as conductors because they permit the free flow of electrons.
3. When electricity travels in a circuit it moves in a current, instead of discharging all at once as with static electricity.

 Materials Needed

1. A wire stripper.
For each group
2. One small bulb. (A #44, 46, or 48 is about the size of a flashlight bulb, is inexpensive, and will last indefinitely if not placed in a series circuit with more than two batteries.)
3. A small bulb holder. (Try to get the kind that come with fahnstock clips because they eliminate the need for screwdrivers.)
4. A screwdriver, if needed.
5. One D cell battery.
6. Three 15 cm lengths of bell wire.
7. One fat rubber band (the kind used to hold broccoli stems together).
8. Two fahnstock clips. (See Getting Started.)

For each child
9. Data sheet and followup sheet.

 Getting Started

1. Before class, slide the two fahnstock clips onto the rubber band for each group. The clips will anchor the wires so that they make contact with the battery terminals.

   Strip about 1½ cm of insulation off both ends of each length of wire.

Exposed wire (the children will thread it through here later)

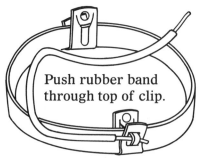

Push rubber band through top of clip.

1. Review the concepts that sound and magnetic energy can travel with varying ability through different materials.

   Elicit that static electricity occurs when electrons jump. Inform your electrical engineers that they are going to create current electricity by discovering how to get electrons to run on a highway called a *circuit*. They will also find out what materials will allow electricity to come aboard the circuit.

   They will know that electricity is running through the circuit in a current when the bulb lights up.

2. Give each group one bulb, one bulb holder (and screwdriver if needed), one battery, and one wire, and challenge them to work cooperatively to try to get the bulb to light up.

   Before actually building the "circuits," they should look carefully at each diagram on the data sheet and indicate their predictions. (Diagrams 2 and 3 will work.)

3. Distribute the rubber bands (with fahnstock clips) and one length of wire, and show the children how to construct a simple circuit for testing the junkpile.

   To connect the wires into the fahnstock clips, tell the children to squeeze the ends of the clip, and they will be able to thread the wire through the metal loop on the side.

Squeeze ends together

Metal loop will appear through slit. Thread end of wire through loop

They should place the rubber band around the battery lengthwise so that the clips are held firmly against the terminals.

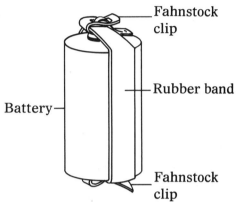

Fahnstock clip

Rubber band

Battery

Fahnstock clip

4. Each time an object allows the electricity to come aboard the circuit, they should note in the conductor table what the object is made of. Each time electricity doesn't flow, they should note in the insulator table the material that blocked it.

5. The children should conclude that metals are good conductors while non-metals function as insulators.

   Check for understanding by holding up a screwdriver and asking why electricians don't use screwdrivers with metal handles, and why they wear rubber-soled shoes.

Electrical Safety Inspector

 Procedure

1. This followup is designed to be "conducted" as a parent-child activity only. It makes a good homework assignment.

   The first rule about keeping appliances away from water will engender many questions about the conductivity of water. Pure water is not a good conductor, but water with salts dissolved from rocks (like most running water) becomes a good conductor.

Emphasize that handling appliances with wet hands is also dangerous.

batteries in it, or two bulbs, or both.

A circuit which has two or more batteries or bulbs in a row is called a *series circuit*. (I liken this term to the World Series or a television series, which has games or programs in a row.)

Strategic Tips

1. When the children are working with batteries, they are handling only 1.5 volts of electricity. Emphasize over and over again that household current can kill, and that any experiments they conduct should be only with D or smaller sized batteries and never with household current.

2. Have your wire stripper handy, because the exposed ends will probably break off several wires.

3. Several children will have trouble completing a circuit because they have pushed their wire too far into the fahnstock clips, so that only the insulated covering makes contact with the clip. Sometimes the rubber bands slip off the terminals, or the clips do not make good contact with the terminals. Always check these connections before assuming the battery has gone dead or the bulb has burnt out.

4. As a followup, you may wish to challenge your more capable students to build a circuit with two

Predict which series circuit will be brightest.

Find out.

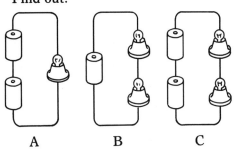

A   B   C

All Aboard

physical

For electrons to travel the circuit, 2 places on the battery must be connected with 2 places on the bulb. You may use 1 wire to help. First predict which of the setups below will make a circuit. Mark C for circuit or N for no circuit.

1. Prediction: _____	**2.** Prediction: _____	**3.** Prediction: _____
4. Prediction: _____	**5.** Prediction: _____	**6.** Prediction: _____

Find the Conductor and let electricty come aboard the circuit! Put a check in the space.

Conductor		Insulator	
Metal	Non-Metal	Metal	Non-Metal

Conductors are _____.

Insulators are _____.

This identifies _____ and _____
(child)   (adult)

as official **Electrical Safety Inspectors**.

Circle Yes (**Y**) or No (**N**) to complete inspection of house.

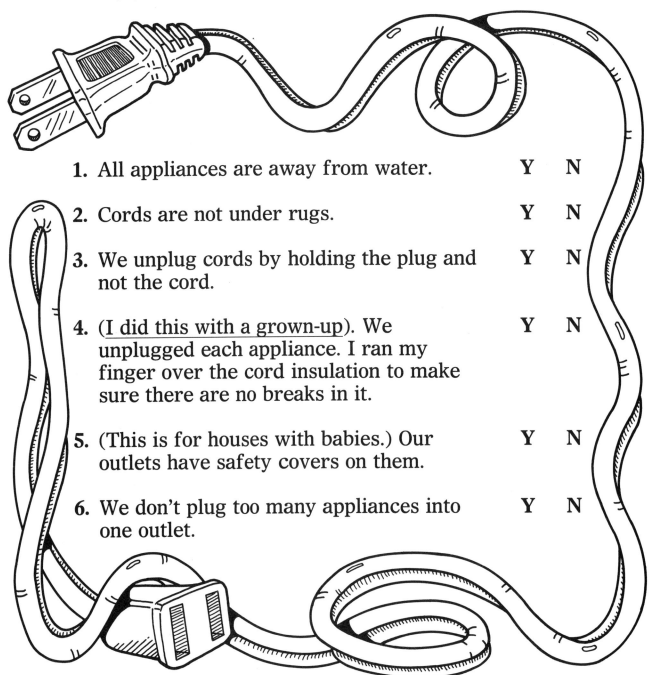

1. All appliances are away from water. Y   N

2. Cords are not under rugs. Y   N

3. We unplug cords by holding the plug and not the cord. Y   N

4. (I did this with a grown-up). We unplugged each appliance. I ran my finger over the cord insulation to make sure there are no breaks in it. Y   N

5. (This is for houses with babies.) Our outlets have safety covers on them. Y   N

6. We don't plug too many appliances into one outlet. Y   N

Make an Electrical Safety Poster:

1. Write 2 or more safety rules on a large piece of paper.

2. Illustrate your rules. BE NEAT and COLORFUL!

Bibliography

Part One: Life Science

Edible Plants

A Book of Vegetables, Harriet Langsam Sobol. 1984. Putnam (3–5)

Apple Tree, Barrie Watts. 1987. Silver (PS–2)

Bean and Plant, Christine Back. 1986. Silver (1–3)

Let's Eat, True Kelly. 1986. Dutton (K–2)

Potatoes, Sylvia A. Johnson. 1984. Lerner (4–7)

Sugaring Time, Kathryn Lasky. 1963. Macmillan (4–7)

Flowers and Their Parts

Discovering Flowering Plants, Jennifer Coldrey. 1987. Watts (2–3)

Flower Finder, May Thielgaard Watts. 1955. Nature Study (for teachers and older children)

Flowers: A Guide to Familiar American Wildflowers, Herbert S. Zim and Alexander C. Martin. 1955. Western Paper (for teachers and older children)

Flowers, Fruits, Seeds, Jerome Wexler. 1988. Prentice-Hall (1–3)

From Flower to Flower: Animals and Pollination, Patricia Lauber. 1987. Crown (2–6)

How A Seed Grows, Helene J. Jordan. 1960. Harper (2–4)

Plant Experiments, Vera Webster. 1982. (Children 1–4)

The Plant Sitter, Gene Zion. 1959. Harper (PS–2)

Plants In Winter, Joanna Cole. 1973. Harper (1–3)

Pumpkin, Pumpkin, Jeanne Titherington. 1986. Greenwillow (PS–1)

Seeds: Pop, Stick, Glide, Patricia Lauber. 1981. Crown (2–5)

The Tiny Seed, Eric Carle. 1987. Picture Book (K–2)

Weeds and Wildflowers, Illa Podendorf, 1981. (Children K–3)

Food Chains and Ecology

A Forest Is Reborn, James R. Newton. 1982. Harper (2–4)

Chains, Webs and Pyramids: The Flow of Energy In Nature, Laurence Pringle. 1975. Harper (4–7)

The Seasons of Arnold's Apple Tree, Gail Gibbons. 1984. Harcourt (PS–1)

The Squirrel In The Trees, Jennifer Coldrey. 1986. Stevens (4–6)

Underground Life, Allan Roberts. 1983. (Children 1–4)

Trees

A Tree Is A Plant, Clyde Robert Bulla. 1960. Harper (K–2)

How Leaves Change, Sylvia A. Johnson. 1986. Lerner (3–5)

Trees, Carolyn Boulton. 1984. Watts (4–6). Has excellent teacher's instructions for forcing buds, leaf collecting, etc.

Trees, Herbert S. Zim and Alexander C. Martin. 1952. Western Paper (for teachers and older children)

Part Two: Earth Science

Astronomy: Earth as a Planet

A Book of Planet Earth For You, Franklyn M. Branley. 1975. Harper (3–5)

North, South, East, West, Franklyn M. Branley. 1966. Harper (1–3)

What Makes Day and Night, Franklyn M. Branley. 1986. Harper (1–3)

The Making of Our Earth

The Beginning of the Earth, Franklyn M. Branley. 1972. Harper (2–4)

Coasts, Keith Lye. 1989. Silver (4–7)

Continents, Dennis B. Fradin. 1986. (Children 1–3)

Earth, Alfred Leutscher. 1983. Dial (K–2)

The Eruption and Healing of Mount St. Helen's, Patricia Lauber. 1986. Bradbury (2–5)

How to Dig a Hole to the Other Side of the World, Faith McNulty. 1979. Harper (PS–3)

The Magic Schoolbus: Inside the Earth, Joanna Cole. 1987. Scholastic (2–5)

Mountain, Lionel Bender. 1989. Watts (3–5)

River, Lionel Bender. 1988. Watts (4–6)

Volcanoes and Earthquakes, Martyn Bramwell. 1986. Watts (2–5)

The Moon

The First Travel Guide to the Moon: What to Pack, How to Go, and What to See When You Get There, Rhoda Blumberg. 1980. Macmillan (4–8)

The Moon, Seymour Simon. 1984. Macmillan (3–6)

What the Moon Is Like, Franklyn M. Branley. 1986. Harper (1–3)

The Planets and the Solar System

The Comet and You, E. C. Krupp. 1985. Macmillan (K–3)

If You Lived On Mars, Melvin Berger. 1988. Dutton (4–6)

The Planets in our Solar System, Franklyn M. Branley. 1987. Harper (2–4)

The Sun, Our Nearest Star, Don Madden. 1988. Harper (1–3)

Sun Up, Sun Down, Gail Gibbons. 1983. Harcourt (1–3)

Rocks and Minerals

A First Look At Rocks, Millicent E. Selsam and Joyce Hunt. 1984. Walker (K–3)

Bibliography (cont.)

Air is All Around You, Franklyn M. Branley. 1986. Harper (PS–6)

The Big Rock, Bruce Hiscock. 1988. Macmillan (1–4)

It's Raining Cats and Dogs: All Kinds of Weather and Why We Have It, Franklyn M. Branley. 1987. Houghton (3–6)

Rock Collecting, Roma Gans. 1984. Harper (1–3)

The Rock Quarry Book, Michael Kehoe. 1981. Carolrhoda (2–3)

Rocks and Minerals, Herbert S. Zim and Paul Schaffer. 1957. Western (for teachers and older children)

Rocks and Minerals, Illa Podendorf. 1982. (Children 1–4)

The Trip of a Drip, Vicki Cobb. 1986. Little (3–5)

What Makes It Rain? The Story of a Raindrop, Keith Brandt. 1982. Troll (1–3)

What Makes the Wind?, Laurence Santrey. 1982. Troll Associates (1–3)

Part Three: Physical Science

Energy: Magnetism and Electricity

Electricity and Magnetism, Kathryn Whyman. 1986. Gloucester (3–6)

Electricity, Mark W. Bailey. 1978. Raintree (2–4)

Energy, Illa Podendorf. 1982. (Children 1–4)

Mickey's Magnet, Franklyn M. Branley and Eleanor K. Vaughn. n.d. Scholastic (K–3)

Switch On, . . . Switch Off, Melvin Berger. 1989. Harper (K–3)

Energy: Sound and Light

Light and Color, L. W. Anderson. 1978. Raintree (2–4)

Shadow Magic, Seymour Simon. 1985. Lothrop (K–3)

Sound and Music, Neil Ardley. 1984. Watts (3–5)

Friction, Heat Energy, and Energy of Motion

Hot and Cold, Irving Adler. 1975. Harper (4–6)

Gravity and Its Effects

Floating and Sinking, Franklyn M. Branley. 1967. Harper (1–3)

Gravity Is A Mystery, Franklyn M. Branley. 1970. Harper (1–3)

Why Doesn't The Earth Fall Up? and Other Not Such Dumb Questions About Motion, Vicki Cobb. 1988. Dutton (2–4)

For Teachers: *Science Matters*, Robert M. Hazen and James Trefil. 1991. Doubleday. This book offers clear, concise explanations of everday scientific phenomena your students are bound to have questions about. It's a great way to refresh your memory of college physics, earth science, and astronomy, as well as to keep abreast of recent developments in science.